LITIGATION-PROOF PATENTS

Avoiding The Most Common
Patent Mistakes

LARRY M. GOLDSTEIN

Published by True Value Press
ISBN-10: 0-9895541-1-2
ISBN-13: 978-0-9895541-1-4

Layout: Marzel A.S. — Jerusalem

Other Books by Larry M. Goldstein

PATENT PORTFOLIOS: Quality, Creation, and Cost [to be published in December, 2014]

TRUE PATENT VALUE: Defining Quality in Patents and Patent Portfolios (published July, 2013)

TECHNOLOGY PATENT LICENSING: An International Reference on 21ˢᵗ Century Patent Licensing, Patent Pools and Patent Platforms (published July, 2004)

Summary Table of Contents

Detailed Table of Contents

Acknowledgments

Thank you to Gil Perlberg and Gal Zuckerman for having reviewed prior drafts. Many of their comments and suggestions have been incorporated, but of course all mistakes remain mine alone.

Thank you to Paz Corcos for her excellent cover graphics, and to A.S. Marzel for his outstanding layout work.

Preface

LITIGATION-PROOF PATENTS

This book is misnamed. The truth is that there is no such thing as a "litigation-proof patent". Many things can happen to a patent as it winds its way from initial application through issuance to litigation and final victory. In the United States, a patent can be weakened or invalidated by the Patent & Trademark Office, by the federal courts, or by the International Trade Commission. The patent statue can be changed by the U.S. Congress in ways that can invalidate patents or render them valid but useless. A "litigation-proof patent" cannot be written, because the thing does not exist and will never exist.

So why pick a name like "Litigation-Proof Patents"? Because this is the standard of quality for which we must all strive. We must keep the ideal in our mind at all times. Even if the ideal cannot be realized in full, we must strive to make our patents as litigation-proof as they can be.

Unfortunately, the majority of patents, I would say the vast majority[1] of patents, do not even approach the ideal, because

---

[1] I do not know exactly how many ICT patents suffer from these defects, but I would estimate that more than 99% of such patents have one or more serious and avoidable problems with quality. To be blunt, virtually all ICT patents are less good than they should have been. Eliminating common

they have one or more serious problems with quality. These are not defects that are unavoidable given the nature of the technology and the patent. Rather, these are mistakes that could have been avoided.

The purpose of this short book is two-fold. First, to identify the principles of top-quality patents — these are the principles that give rise to patents that are as "litigation-proof" as they can be. Second, to identify and define the ten most common mistakes that prevent patents from being "litigation-proof", and to explain how these mistakes may be avoided.

A FEW GENERAL COMMENTS

Here are a few general comments to help readers understand this book.

First, the comparative judgments rendered in this book are my own. For example, the errors I have called "the ten most common patent mistakes" exist without any doubt, but that they are indeed "the most common" mistakes is simply my belief. Similarly, I have listed what I consider to be the single most common, the second most common, and the third most common, mistakes in the writing and prosecuting of patents. I have no external evidence that these are indeed the first, second, and third most common mistakes, but that is my estimate.

Second, the world of patents is generally divided into two broad groups, which are those based primarily on physics,

----

patent mistakes, in particular avoiding the ten common mistakes discussed in this book, would boost patent quality, and would lead to greater scope of claim coverage and/or enhanced resistance against attacks on claim validity.

and those based primarily on biology or chemistry. The first group is typically referenced as "ICT" patents, an acronym for "Information & Communication Technologies". The second group is typically referenced as "BCP" patents, an acronym for "Biotechnology, Chemical, and Pharmaceutical". Generally, any patents that are not BCP patents are automatically classified ICT patents. ICT is therefore considered to include information patents, electronic communication patents, mechanical patents, business methods, and software patents.

Third, the focus of this book is ICT patents, not BCP patents. My background is in physics and electronic communications, and I have no particular expertise in BCP patents. Further, although it is certainly true that basic principles of patent quality, and the most common mistakes in patents, apply to both ICT and BCP patents, nevertheless there are differences between these two groups which would require caution in applying the material here to BCP patents.

Fourth, I believe very strongly in the importance of patent quality. I believe that high-quality patents are of great value both to the holders of the patents and to society as a whole. I believe also that poor-quality patents are, for the most part, a waste of time and money. To help improve the quality of patents, I have written three books, which I call collectively "The Patent Quality Series". The first book of this trilogy, published in July, 2013, is entitled *TRUE PATENT VALUE: Defining Quality in Patents and Patent Portfolios*. (From this point on, *TRUE PATENT VALUE* will be referenced as "*TPV*".) *TPV* discusses in detail about 50 patents, with an emphasis on "high quality" rather than on errors or mistakes.

The current book, *LITIGATION-PROOF PATENTS*,

is the second book in The Patent Quality Series. This book supplements *TPV*. Whereas *TPV* focuses on "high-quality patents", the current book focuses on the most common mistakes that prevent patents from being "high-quality" or "litigation-proof". To understand and avoid these common mistakes is a prerequisite to creating "high-quality" patents, and hence a prerequisite to maximizing the financial value of a patent.

The third book in The Patent Quality Series is ***PATENT PORTFOLIOS: Quality, Creation, and Cost***. Building on the principles of "true value" and "avoiding common mistakes", the third book defines "excellent patent portfolio", explains how to create such a portfolio, and presents the most common methods for budgeting to obtain such a portfolio. The creation of an excellent patent portfolio should be the ultimate goal of any company or innovator interested in protecting innovation and creating value in patents. Hence, the third book, ***PATENT PORTFOLIOS***, **is** the culmination of the series started in ***TRUE PATENT VALUE*** and continued in ***LITIGATION-PROOF PATENTS***.

CHAPTER SUMMARIES

CHAPTER 1 presents fundamental information about patents. There are two topics.

1. Although a patent is a legal document, it is also a story. It tells about the current state of a technology, it explains a certain invention that was discovered and developed, and it makes claim to at least part of the invention. Chapter 1 discusses how that story is told, in particular the parts of a patent that have a major

impact on the quality of the story and that are subject to mistakes in the telling of the story.

2. Chapter 1 explains what I consider to be the most effective and efficient way to write a patent application. This is the method that is, in my opinion, the most likely to capture the essence of the invention, and the least likely to include common patent mistakes.

CHAPTER 2 presents and discusses the principles of patent quality in the following groups:

1. Characteristics of Good Patent Claims.
2. Key Claim Terms.
3. Types of Claims.
4. Patent Value.
5. Seminal Patents.
6. Tips for Writing Patent Applications.

CHAPTER 3 lists what I consider to be the ten most common mistakes in ICT patents. Each mistake is identified, and then explained with an example. For some of these mistakes, simply to understand the mistake is to understand also how to avoid it, but in some cases I provide additional explanation for avoiding the mistake. Several of the mistakes appear so frequently, even in otherwise outstanding patents, that I call these mistakes "the most common mistake", "the second most common mistake", and "the third most common mistake", respectively. Here is the list of common mistakes:

1. *The Most Common Mistake:* Unclear Key Claim Terms.
2. *The Second Most Common Mistake:* Roads Not Taken.
3. *The Third Most Common Mistake:* Defective Parallelism.
4. Unnecessary Limitation in the Written Description.
5. Improper Use of Claim Differentiation.

6. Lack of Claim Mix.
7. Improper Mix of Elements Within a Claim.
8. Improper Use of Non-Standard Terminology.
9. Incorrect Reliance on the Preamble.
10. External Events that Destroy Patent Value.

CHAPTER 4 presents three examples of "litigation-proof patents" taken from the 20th and 21st centuries. Each example includes identification and explanation of patent mistakes that could have been avoided.

1. Beauty, Brains, and Patents in World War II: The Hedy Lamarr Patent (1942).
2. Does a Patent Give a Monopoly on Monopoly®? (1935).
3. Apple v. Samsung: The "Slide to Unlock" Patent (2011).

Chapter 4 ends with Table 4–5, which is a comparison of all the patents presented in the chapter against the ten most common patent mistakes.

Chapter 1

The Fundamentals of Patents

INTRODUCTION TO CHAPTER 1

Chapter 1 deals with two aspects fundamental to the rest of this book.

First, every patent tells a story. This section focuses on how exactly a patent tells its story. Highlighted are those sections of a patent which tell the story — no attempt is made to describe every part of a patent, but rather only those parts that tell the story.

Second, a method is described in detail by which a litigation-proof patent may be written. Other people may use other methods, but in my opinion, the method described here is the most effective and efficient way of writing a patent that tells the story and creates maximum value.

THE STORY TOLD BY A PATENT

The many different parts of a patent can be confusing, but the essence of a patent is clear. In one way or another, a patent explains:

(1)   The current state of a technology (that is, what came before an invention),

(2)   The invention in various embodiments, and

(3)   The part of the invention for which legal protection is sought.

If this story is well-told, then the patent is high-quality. But if there are gaps in the story, contradictions, discussions in wrong places, unexplained diversions, or other problems of narrative, the patent has been badly written and the story cannot be understood.

(1) The current state of the technology should be discussed briefly in the section called "Background" or "Background of the Invention". It should not be discussed anywhere else in the patent. In fact, discussion of background technology outside of the Background section will create confusion as to what part of the described technology is included within the background (often called "prior art") and what part of such technology is included within various embodiments of the invention. The background technology must be discussed only in the Background section.[2]

---

[2] Of course the discussion of invention embodiments in the Detailed Description or other sections of the patent will explain how the invention works with reference to technology that already exists. In this sense, description of the invention will necessarily rely on existing technology. However, this discussion will not create confusion between "background technology"

Similarly, the "Background" section must include only background technology and nothing connected with the invention — no parts of the innovation and no embodiments may be place in the "Background". Unfortunately, this rule is sometimes broken, definitions or other parts of the invention sometimes appear in the Background, and the result is that there is confusion between background technology and the invention.[3]

(2) The invention in its various embodiments is described in several specific sections of the patent. These sections include:

— *Title* or "*Title of Invention*": The Title is the first thing seen by evaluators. It therefore creates the first impression on the reader. Hopefully, the Title accurately captures the general subject.[4]

---

and "the invention embodiments". The confusion can arise only if there is a general discussion of background technology outside of the Background section, at which point readers will not understand what is background technology and what is part of the invention. Although this mistake — discussing background technology outside of the Background section — does occur in patents, it is not particularly common. Far more common is the mistake of incorrectly including within the Background section Key Claim Terms, definitions of such terms, or discussion of invention embodiments, This incorrect inclusion of invention material within the Background is a mistake that should never occur, but it happens not infrequently.

[3] A well-written Background of Invention does *not* describe the invention, but may describe the problem that is solved by the invention, and in that way help explain the nature of the invention. Evaluators reviewing a patent for possible commerce will often look at the Background, so a clear statement here can help communicate your invention to interested parties, and in that way increase patent value. People will not pay money to buy or license-in patents they do not understand.

[4] In theory, an incorrect or narrow title could limit the scope of the

— *Abstract*: The Abstract summarizes the invention, or at least some embodiments of the invention, in a few words.

— *Field of Invention*, sometimes called *"Field of Technology"* or simply *"Field"*: This section is optional, and if it appears at all, it will be a very short statement of the general technical area of the patent.[5]

— *Summary of the Invention* or *"Brief Summary"* or just *"Summary"*: Like the Abstract, the Summary is also a relatively brief summary of the invention, but the Summary is typically longer, and should describe, in brief, every embodiment of the invention that might be claimed now or in the future.

— *Brief Description of the Drawings*: Each figure is described very briefly, typically with no more than a single sentence. For example, "Fig. 4 is a top-down view of an apparatus for use in the storage of electronic information". The key in this section is not to write anything that could limit the scope of the invention. The example just given might be better if it were written

---

invention. I am not aware of any court that has so ruled, but it could happen, because the title is part of the written description of the invention.

[5] For such a short section, the Field of Invention can be surprisingly difficult to write. It should not be overly broad, which could invite an examiner or a court to expand the range of possible prior art applicable against the claims, nor should it be too narrow, which might be used by a court to limit the scope of the invention. Because of its problematic nature, the Field of Invention is often left out. Nevertheless, the Field of Invention may be useful to communicate quickly the general area of the patent. Also, some patent practitioners may use the Field of Invention to direct the patent application to particular examination groups within the PTO. See Robert D. Fish, *Strategic Patenting*, (Trafford Publishing, Victoria, British Colombia, Canada, 2007), at pp.207–209.

thus: "Fig. 4 is a top-down view of an apparatus for storing or communicating information". The second form includes both "storing" and "communicating". The second form is not limited to "electronic" information.

— *Detailed Description*, sometimes called *"Detailed Description of the Invention"*: This is the main description of the invention, and usually it will take up substantially more than 50% of the entire patent. The Detailed Description defines the invention, and every embodiment, in great detail. Most of the Detailed Description will be a discussion of every figure in the patent. Every element in every figure must be described. Each part of the invention that is new, what I call each "Point of Novelty" (or "PON"), must be described very clearly in the patent, and that is typically done in the Detailed Description.

Of all the sections of the patent, the Detailed Description has the greatest potential for explaining the invention. Unfortunately, the Detailed Description also has great potential for including avoidable mistakes, in particular, the two most common mistakes — Unclear Key Claim Terms, and Roads Not Taken. The Detailed Description is therefore a vitally important section of litigation-proof patents.

Finally, a word to avoid confusion. There are two sections in the patent that include the word "description", which are the "Brief Description of the Drawings" and the "Detailed Description of the Invention". However, the patent is explained by all of the sections that have substantive material, including the Title, Abstract, Field of Invention, Summary, Brief Description of the Drawings, Detailed Description, and finally the Background as a contrast to the innovative concepts. A good patent will have a match between terms used in the claims and the explanation of those terms throughout the entire "written description", including all of the sections just listed. In this book, I make reference to the "written description" to include all of the sections of the patent that explain the invention, its embodiments, and the key terms used in the patent.[6]

— *Figures*: The figures are diagrams and flow charts rather than descriptive narrative. They work hand in hand with the Detailed Description. Every element in every figure should be discussed in the Detailed Description. There should be at least one figure for each independent claim[7] in the patent. Some patents include one or more figures describing background technology, which

---

6 Each of the individual sections "describes" a particular aspect of the invention, but not the entire invention nor all of its embodiments. In contrast, the patent term "written description" is used here to mean a combination of all of the individual narratives which make up, collectively, the explanation of the patent, its embodiments, and key terms. If I mean a specific section of the patent, then I will note that section by name and with capitalization, such as "Detailed Description". However, if I mean the entire body of the patent describing the invention, I will use the phrase "written description". It should be understood that although "Background" is included within "written description", the Background section is used solely to introduce the general topic and indicate the problems existing in the technology, but definitely *not* to state embodiments of the invention. It should be understood that "written description" includes also the description of each element in each of the figures.

7 An "independent claim" is a claim that stands on its own. It does not depend on any other claim. In every patent, claim #1 is always independent, and other claims may be independent. If, however, a claim makes a specific reference to an earlier claim, then the referring claim is "dependent". For example, consider claim #1. "A plant", and claim #2, "Claim 1, further comprising a flower". Claim #1 is independent, whereas claim #2 is dependent on #1, and claim #2 includes a plant with a flower.

is acceptable provided that the figure is clearly marked as "Prior Art" or "Background Technology".

There are many other sections of the patent relating to time of filing, time of issuance, inventors, priority dates, ownership, and many other factors, and these sections are important, but they do not relate to the telling of the patent story.

(3) The background technology and the written description tell the patent's story, but they do not set the bounds of legal protection. Rather, the claims define the legal protection. The claims are a vitally important part of the patent. In 1990, a well-known patent judge wrote what has become a famous line in the patent world, "The name of the game is the claim."[8] The intent of this quote is two-fold. First, it is ultimately the claims (together with the written description supporting the claims) that determine the value of the patent. Second, as a result, the scope of legal protection afforded by the patent can only be as broad as the patent claims. The scope can be narrower, and it often is narrower due to the many mistakes in patents that are discussed in this book, but the scope may never be broader than the claims of the issued patent.

Although the claims and the written description work together closely, nevertheless there is a fundamental difference between these two. The written description and the figures are for the most part fixed at the time the application is

---

8 Giles S. Rich, formerly the Chief Judge of what was then the sole appellate court in the United States for patent decisions of lower federal courts, The Extent of the Protection and Interpretation of Claims — American Perspective, 21 Int'l Rev. Indus. Prop. & Copyright L., 497, 499 (1990).

filed. Minor corrections may be made, but any basic change, or the addition of substantive new material, will create a new filing date (at least as to the changed or added material). Since the maintenance of an early filing date is critically important to the value of the patent, creation of a new filing date often reduces, sometimes drastically, the value of the patent. For this reason, it is generally considered by patent drafters and patent owners that the written description and the figures are fixed on the date of initial filing.

However, whereas the written description is relatively static, the claims are fluid. While the patent application is pending, the claims represent the legal protection that the owner wants. When the patent issued, the claims represent the legal protection permitted by the patent office — this is to say, the allowed claims determine the protection that the owner actually receives. The claims as filed and the claims as issued are often dramatically different, and the differences are caused by what is called the "patent prosecution process" between the applicant and the patent office. This is the process by which claims are presented, the patent office reacts, the applicant responds, the patent office reacts again, etc., until the two parties have reached agreement on the claims that will be issued.[9] Since the claims as issued are determined both by the claims as filed and by what happens to the filed claims

---

[9] The interaction between the applicant and the patent office is written, and this written record is called the "file history" of the patent. The file history consists primarily of filings by the applicant, "Office Actions" by the patent office, and "responses to Office Action" by the applicant. In many cases, before a patent is allowed the patent examiner will write a statement called "Notice of Allowance" which includes the "reasons for allowance", and that, too, will be part of the record. The file history is not physically part of the published patent, but it is nevertheless an integral part of the interpretation of the patent.

during prosecution, it is clear that all of the mistakes discussed in this book that are focused specifically on the claims can occur either during patent drafting or during patent prosecution. As just one example, contradictions between what appears in the Detailed Description and what appears in the claims may occur either during the drafting of the original patent application or by changes made to the claims during prosecution. I do not distinguish in this book by the stage at which an error is made. Rather, I focus only on avoidable mistakes, whenever they are made.[10]

WRITING A PATENT APPLICATION

After an innovative concept has been created and developed, a patent application may be written to explain and protect the concept. There are different ways to write a patent application, but I consider a particular method to be both optimally effective (that is, capturing the entire invention and all of its embodiments) and efficient (that is, drafting the application with the most reasonable amount of time and effort). I present here a table of the steps, and I will then explain each step in the method.

---

[10] It makes no legal difference whether a mistake was made during drafting or during prosecution. As a practical matter, the entire process of drafting is within the sole control of the applicant, so avoidable mistakes made during drafting are the sole responsibility of the applicant or the applicant's attorney. In contrast, so many different things can happen during prosecution that mistakes made at this stage, while still avoidable, are much more understandable. In any case, this book is not about prosecution or the differences between writing and prosecuting patent applications. This distinction will not be discussed further.

Table 1–1: The Steps for Writing a Patent Application

1. Define **Points of Novelty**

2. Plan, then write, **independent claims**

3. Plan, then write, **dependent claims and figures**

4. Identify, then explain, the Key Claim Terms ("**KCTs**")

5. Write general sections — **Title, Field of Invention, Background, Summary, Abstract**

6. Write **Brief Description** of figures

7. Write **Detailed Description** of figures, and explain every KCT

8. **Review entire application**: Verify that common mistakes have been avoided

Step 1 Points of Novelty: Start at the end. That is the way to do it.

Before you write anything, you must understand what it is you wish to protect. I call these the "Points of Novelty", or "PONs". Points of Novelty are the aspects of the invention that (1) you think are innovations, and (2) you want to cover with independent claims.

The identification of the Points of Novelty must be the starting point of the patent application. You need to know where the patent will end before you start writing. Only after you know where you are going can you begin the process of writing.[11]

According to one's philosophy of patent writing, additional actions could be part of Step 1, although the ultimate goal is to end with the PONs to be claimed in the application. For example, many patent professionals recommend that a prior art search be performed before any drafting. The goal of a prior art search would be two-fold:

First, to understand clearly what already exists, and to use this knowledge to define the Points of Novelty most closely associated with the various embodiments disclosed by the inventor. If a concept that the patentee thought was a Point of Novelty already exists in the prior art, then the PON is in fact not novel, and should not be claimed. Alternatively, a particular aspect or embodiment of the PON may exist in the prior art, but the PON may still be viable if it is modified to avoid prior art.

---

[11] Or in the words of the old adage, "If you don't know where you are going, any road will get you there." This was supposedly the advice given by the Cheshire Cat to Alice. However, the Cheshire Cat never said this. The actual exchange, in Chapter 6 of Lewis Carroll's *Alice in Wonderland*, is:

> "Would you tell me, please, which way I ought to go from here?"
> "That depends a good deal on where you want to get to," said the Cat.
> "I don't much care where —" said Alice.
> "Then it doesn't matter which way you go," said the Cat.
> "— so long as I get SOMEWHERE," Alice added as an explanation.
> "Oh, you're sure to do that," said the Cat, "if you only walk long enough."

I prefer the actual exchange to the commonly stated misquote. If you write a patent application without knowing where you want to arrive, then you will indeed arrive SOMEWHERE, but you may not be happy when you get there. That is to say, if you don't know what it is you want to protect in the patent, then you truly do not know where the patent will end up, and you are wasting your time with a patent application. To define the PONs is the first thing you must do before writing a patent application.

Second, to understand specifically what does *not* exist in the prior art, and then to expand the patentable concepts to their maximum scope possible, *even if the expansion is not part of the inventor's original embodiments*. The claims will then include the inventor's embodiments, and also viable alternatives that the inventor perhaps did not consider and which perhaps the inventor does not plan to implement with actual products and services. This is to say, the patent claims may be broader than the product plans of the inventor. One patent attorney has called this "market-oriented" rather than "invention-oriented" patent claiming, or "white space patenting".[12]

Prior art, including the search of prior art, is a very extensive topic that is not discussed further in this book. For present purposes, it is important to understand that any prior processes of innovation, and any prior art searching, must ultimately end with a clear understanding of the Points of Novelty. This understanding is the objective and the end of Step 1 of the method for drafting a patent application.[13]

---

[12] The concept of "market-oriented" patent claiming is to identify alternative solutions and embodiments in the technical area of the invention which have not been claimed or even disclosed by any competitor in the market. If the claims in the current application can capture the future direction of the market, the patent can become extremely valuable. This concept has also been called "white space patenting", in the sense that the inventor and the patent drafter must identify the "white spaces" in the market that have not been claimed, and then cover those spaces in the new patent. See Robert D. Fish, *White Space Patenting: "Patenting Ideas, Not Just Inventions"*, (Fish & Associates, Irvine, CA, November, 2013).

[13] In a certain sense, the patent is the culmination of the process started with the invention. One could therefore say that the invention and the patent are part of the same process. It would be possible to write a book on both innovation and patenting, but this book focuses solely on the latter. Similarly, some people feel that the search for prior art should also be considered part

Step 2 — Independent claims: Having defined the Points of Novelty, the necessary second step is to plan the independent claims. Each PON must have at least one independent claim[14], and every independent claim should have only one PON.[15] Beyond that, what kind(s) of independent claim(s) do you want for each Point of Novelty? Do you want "structure claims", or "method claims", or both?[16] If you want "structure claims", what kind of structure claims — "system", "device", or "component"? You may choose to have different kinds of independent claims for the same PON. If so, do you wish to maximize patent protection for this PON by the technique known as "claim parallelism"?[17] Once you have decided the

---

of the same process of innovation and patenting. The process of searching for and reviewing prior art — the reasons for doing so, when it should be done or not done, how to do it, the results of the search, and other aspects — is an interesting and important topic, but it is not part of the current book.

[14] If a PON does not have at least one independent claim, then you have decided that it is not a PON after all. A Point of Novelty is an innovation you have decided to cover with a claim.

[15] Having two or more Points of Novelty in a single independent claim is a mistake, because this multiplicity unnecessarily limits the scope of the claim. If there are multiple PONs, then have a separate independent claim for each one. You may, if you wish, plan to capture some of the Points of Novelty described not in the first application, but rather in a continuation application. However, your general intent should be to claim each Point of Novelty at some point in time, and each PON should be captured by one or more of its own independent claims.

[16] Please do not be confused by thinking, "I have only a method claim", or "I have only a structure claim". The line between method claims and structure claims is often extremely thin. In many cases, in fact I would say the great majority of cases, it is possible to state the same Point of Novelty as a method or as a structure, or as both. Techniques for converting claims from one type to another are discussed in Chapter 7 of *TPV* and in other patent literature.

[17] "Claim parallelism" is discussed in Chapter 3. It is one technique, and in my opinion it is the single strongest technique, to maximize patent protection for a single Point of Novelty. However, the technique of claim

independent claims you want for the Points of Novelty, write a first draft of these claims.

Step 3 — Dependent claims and figures: The next step is to draft the dependent claims, and complete the figures. I write the step in this way, because neither the dependent claims nor the figures are prerequisites for one another, but they must both be finished before going on to the next step. Thus it is possible to do the dependent claims first, or conversely the figures first.

For the dependent claims, ask yourself, "What features or aspects could be added that would increase the usefulness or value of the independent claim? Which of these features or aspects have higher priority?" The higher priority features or aspects will become the elements in the dependent claims. In many patents, the same features or aspects become dependent claims for two or more of the independent claims — this is not mandatory, but it is entirely sensible. The usual problem with writing dependent claims is not a shortage of ideas but rather an excess — in most cases, you will need to select which of many options you want to embody in the dependent claims.

For drafting figures, there are some basic rules. First, every patent needs at least one structure figure and one method figure. No exceptions to this rule — *your patent must have at least one structure figure and one method figure.*

Second, every independent method claim must be supported by at least one method figure and one structure figure. The method figure will show the specific steps of the

---

parallelism must be applied correctly — incorrect application of the technique is "defective parallelism", and is the third most common mistake in patents, as explained in Chapter 3.

independent method claim. Every independent method claim should have its own method figure, because the method is different in each such claim. The structure figure will show at least one structure that supports execution of the method. One structure figure may support two or more method claims. By "support", I mean you must be able to say, "The method in independent claim __ could operate on the structure shown in Fig. X." It is not necessary to make this statement in the patent, but it necessary that you could make the statement if needed, because the statement demonstrates that the method is indeed supported by structure.

Third, for structure claims, each independent structure claim must be supported by a structure figure. Usually that is as far as it goes. It is possible to go farther, however, and say "The structural elements in structure claim C may support the method shown in figure Y".

Let us summarize these relationships in a table.[18]

Table 1–2: Figure Requirements for Independent Claims

Type of Independent Claim	Is a Figure required for this claim?	Is a supporting Figure required for this claim?
Method	Yes, a method figure is required.	Yes, a structure figure is required.
Structure	Yes, a structure figure is required.	No, not required. A method figure is optional only.

---

[18] Everything said here applies only to Information & Communication Technologies ("ICT") patents. It is likely that most of the comments herein apply also to Biotechnology, Chemical, and Pharmaceutical ("BCP") patents, but there may be variations or nuances for BCP patents of which I am unaware, so I make no comment as to BCP patents.

Step 4 — Identify and Define Key Claim Terms: Having written a first draft of all the claims and all the figures, the next step is to plan the written description. First, identify the Key Claim Terms ("KCTs") in the claims, and make absolutely certain, 100% certain, that each KCT is adequately explained in the written description. A "Key Claim Term" is a word or phrase appearing in a claim that helps define the nature or scope of a claim. In fact, the claim cannot be understood without a clear understanding of the KCTs appearing in the claim. The failure to explain the Key Claim Terms is the single most common mistake in patents, and occurs in the majority of ICT patents.[19]

A KCT can be explained in any or all of three ways.[20]

(1)   Write a definition of the KCT, either in the Summary or more likely in the Detailed Description. This is my personal preference.

(2)   Give multiple examples of possible implementations of the KCT — a simple list of options is the usual presentation.

(3)   Show the KCT as an element in a figure, and explain the element in the Detailed Description.

Each of the three techniques has advantages and disadvantages. These can be displayed graphically.

---

[19]   Every patent explains some of its KCTs, but very few explain correctly all of their KCTs. That is, the vast majority of ICT patents either fail to explain, or explain incorrectly, one or more KCTs. In patent litigation, "close enough" is simply not acceptable, because a single unclear Key Claim Term can destroy an entire patent.

[20]   The fourth way of explaining a KCT, "claim differentiation", is for a court, and should never be relied upon by a patent writer. A patent writer's deliberate reliance on claim differentiation to explain a KCT is one of the common mistakes discussed in Chapter 3.

Table 1–3: Techniques for Explaining Key Claim Terms

Type of Technique	Main Advantage	Main Disadvantage
(1) Definition	Great control[21]	Tends to be abstract
(2) List of examples	Easily understood options	Definitional boundary unclear
(3) Element in a figure	Easiest to grasp quickly	Only one example (and may therefore be limited)

The strongest explanation of a KCT uses some combination of (1) definitions, (2) examples, and (3) figure elements. In some cases, all three techniques are used to explain a term, which is a very powerful combination (provided, of course, that there are no contradictions between or among the explanations of the different techniques).

The identification of Key Claim Terms will occur also at the very beginning, in Step 1, as part of the clarification of the Points of Novelty. However, in my experience it is almost impossible to capture all the PONs prior to writing the claims — new concepts are developed, different ideas are merged, certain concepts may be expanded, etc. Additional terms of importance are likely to arise during the drafting of the claims. Hence, the Key Claim Terms should be identified and explained in Step 4, after the claims have been written and the figures created.

---

21 By law, a patent writer is his or her own lexicographer. Within certain reasonable limits, the patent writer may define terms used in the patent in ways most suited to enhance the scope and validity of the claims.

Step 5 — Write the General Sections: The next step is to draft the five general sections of the patent, which are, solely in the order in which they appear in a patent draft, the Title, the Field of Invention, the Background, the Summary, and the Abstract. Of these sections, the Title, Field, Summary, and Abstract relate to the invention and its embodiments, whereas the Background acts as a foil to these other sections.

However, probably the main function of all these sections is not to describe the invention in detail, but rather to give to patent evaluators and other readers a very quick and yet accurate view of what the patent is about. Patent evaluators analyzing a portfolio (particularly a relatively large portfolio of hundreds of items, or more) typically spend very little time on the preliminary review of any individual patent — often two minutes or less. If evaluators can grasp quickly the story of the patent, and if they find the story interesting, they will invest more time. But if they cannot understand the essence of the story within this short time, they are likely to move on to the next patent. Evaluators almost always review these five general sections, even in the quickest review, and therefore these sections form the drafter's best chance to communicate quickly with readers of the patent.

The Title of the patent must be short, descriptive of the general area of the invention, and sufficiently broad to cover both the embodiments to be claimed in the current patent and any other embodiments from this invention that may be claimed in the future. However, the Title must not be so broad as to invite prior art searching from unrelated technical areas. In my experience, the drafting of the Title is a moderately difficult task.

The Field of Invention, by contrast, is often very difficult to draft. This section is optional, and it is often omitted, perhaps due to the difficulty in drafting it. Like the Title, the Field is short and descriptive, but by necessity the Field will include the general area of both the invention and the background technology. It is the balance of the competing needs to both (1) broaden the subject of the patent, and also (2) restrict the scope of relevant prior art that may be applied against the claims, which often makes the Field surprisingly hard to write.

For the Background, state the area of the patent, and explain the relevant aspects of the current state of the technology. It is acceptable to state limitations or drawbacks in the current technology that the invention will resolve, but you should *never* state solutions or Points of Novelty in the Background section. Mixing current technology with Points of Novelty from the invention is a serious mistake, because the reader can never be certain what is part of the Background (hence prior art) and what is part of the invention. Similarly, do not define any Key Claim Term in the Background section, since this also can create confusion.[22] The Background section should be very short and to-the-point, focused solely on current technology, with no discussion or even reference to the invention or any of the embodiments described in the patent.

For the Summary, two different approaches are commonly used. Both of these approaches are acceptable, and indeed, some people use both approaches in a single Summary. One approach is simply to explain in brief, or "summarize", the

---

[22] I have seen many times a definition or explanation in the Background section that is later used as a key term in the claims. Why do such a thing? Confusion will almost certainly result. Rather, explain KCTs in the Summary or in the Detailed Description, not in the Background.

operation, structure, and key benefits, of various implementations of the invention. The other approach is to restate all the independent claims in a modified and abbreviated form.

For purposes of putting readers on notice, the first approach — general summary — is probably superior,[23] since it intends to summarize several key aspects of the invention. For purposes of providing clear support in the written description for the claims, the second approach — restatement of the independent claims — is preferred.[24] As noted, some patent writers use both approaches in the summary.

For the Abstract, the only real purpose for this section is to put people on notice about the subject of the patent, that is, to make them aware of what is claimed. People who evaluate patents for any reason[25] will read the Abstract with care, and the Abstract is therefore the best single chance to explain the patent to readers. The Abstract should summarize a single central Point of Novelty, or at most two Points of Novelty, in

---

[23] Many evaluators of patents read only the general sections — the Title, Abstract, Summary, Field of Invention, and perhaps Background — together with the independent claims. A reader who cannot grasp the essence of the invention in that material is likely to drop this patent and move on to the next one. For purposes of capturing the reader's interest and attention, the first approach for the Summary — a brief explanation — is best. For more information, see Chapter 2 of *TPV*.

[24] Further, some people try not to make any revelation in the Summary. They are afraid that whatever is not included in the Summary will be excluded, or that a misstatement in the Summary may limit the entire invention. That is another reason to use the second approach to the Summary.

[25] Who evaluates a patent? (1) A person seeking to buy or license the patent. (2) A person against whom a patent has been asserted for infringement. (3) A competitor who wishes to avoid infringement. (4) A person doing due diligence on a company being bought or sold, that owns the patent. (5) A court or a jury in litigation. (6) Anyone interested in doing business with the patent owner, as either a friend or an enemy, may evaluate the patent.

words and phrases that can be understood quickly. This is vitally important. If people cannot understand the patent, it simply has no value.[26]

The order given here for the general sections — Title, Field, Background, Summary, and Abstract — is the order in which these sections typically appear in an application submitted to the patent office. In my opinion, it is critically important to complete the prior steps — Points of Novelty, claims, figures, and Key Claim Terms — before any of the general sections are drafted. However, once the prior steps have been completed, the drafter has sufficient information and understanding to write all of the five general sections, and the particular order of drafting the general sections is not, in my mind, of major importance.

Others disagree. At least one patent attorney feels that the order of drafting the general sections should be Summary => Abstract => Title => Background (placement of Field of Invention unspecified, but presumably between Title and Background).[27] The rationales for this order are (1) first, that the Summary is in large part a rewording of the claims in layman's language; (2) second, that the Summary is relatively narrow followed by a broader Abstract followed by an even broader Title; and (3) third, that the Background is simply a straw man problem that will necessarily be solved by embodi-

---

[26] The converse may or may not be true. That is, if people understand the patent, they might see its value, or they might conclude that it lacks value. The understanding of evaluators is a necessary but not sufficient condition to unlock the patent's value.

Also, it is not necessary that every evaluator understand the patent, but at least some of the evaluators — potential licensees, a potential buyer, or a court — must understand the patent for it to have value.

[27] *White Space Patenting* at pp.193–194.

ments of the invention, so the embodiments must clearly be understood before the Background can be written.[28] I do not disagree with this order of the general sections, but I think the final order of drafting these general sections is a matter of personal preference.

Step 6 — Write the Brief Description: At this point, you have a draft of all the claims, all figures, and all general sections of the patent. The next step is to write the Brief Description, in which you describe briefly each figure — don't use any language that could limit the scope of a figure.

Step 7 — Write the Detailed Description: To complete the application, draft the Detailed Description. In my opinion, the Detailed Description should start with a "definitions section", in which each Key Claim Term is defined. Alternatively, definitions of KCTs may be distributed throughout the Detailed Description where each term arises, rather than in a concentrated section. Nevertheless, I favor a "definitions section", because it (1) gives the writer total control over the explanation of the KCTs, and (2) insures that every term identified as a Key Claim Term will be properly defined in the written description.[29]

---

28 *Ibid.*

29 The addition of a "definitions section" or "glossary" to the Detailed Description section of ICT patents is the subject of a pilot program launched by the U.S. Patent Office on June 2, 2014. See http://www.uspto.gov/patents/init_events/glossary_initiative.jsp. Although I consider the addition of such a "definitions section" to be superior practice, the ultimate results of this pilot program are not yet clear, and the truth is that only a minority of ICT patents have a section for definitions in the Detailed Description. The most common alternative approach, that is, to define terms as they arise in the application, is possible, but carries the risk that one or more Key Claim

With or without an introductory "definitions section", the Detailed Description starts in one of two ways. Some people write a short synopsis of the patent (1–3 paragraphs), followed by discussion of figures. Conversely, some people jump immediately into discussion of the figures, without a synopsis. A synopsis at the start of the Detailed Description is fine as long as it does not limit the scope of the claims. If a synopsis is partially or even wholly redundant to what was said in the Summary or the Abstract, that is also fine, as long as there is no contradiction between the synopsis and the rest of the patent.

The bulk of the Detailed Description should be a discussion of each figure. Every element of every figure must be explained, at least briefly. In the explanation of the figure elements, people often define or give examples of terms that arise. In fact, we could summarize the Detailed Description by saying that its essence, and by far the bulk of the Detailed Description, is an explanation of each element of each figure, combined with explanations (by explicit definition or by a list of examples) for each Key Claim Term or other important word in the patent. The purpose of the Detailed Description is to explain as many possible embodiments of the invention as possible, avoiding language that could limit the scope of the claims, and adding language that could expand the scope of the claims.

After the explanations of figure elements and other terms, some people summarize each claim in the Detailed

---

Terms will not be identified or will otherwise simply not be defined in the patent. *This happens all the time in ICT patents — people frequently fail to define one or more KCTs.* We will see several example of this mistake in the patents analyzed in Chapter 4 below.

Description. The intention is to provide very clear support for the claims in the written description. In some cases, specific claims are stated in the alternative, not in ways in which the claims appear but rather in ways in which they might have appeared — this formulation tends to both expand the scope of claims, and set the stage for continuation applications in the future. However, the summarization of claims in the Detailed Description occurs in only a minority of ICT patents.

Some patents include, typically toward the end of the Detailed Description, a discussion of various usages of the invention. I have seen a list as long as 20 different usages, but whatever the number, each usage must be described in enough detail so that the described usage may support one or more independent claims. Further, if usages are discussed, it is important to add as many as reasonably possible. A very limited number of usages, such as one or two, may lead a court to include that the patent is limited to only these particular usages. In most ICT patents there is no list of usages, but when such a list does appear, it can be a very useful tool to expand the scope of the described invention. In place of a single list of usages as the end of the Detailed Description, some patents distribute a number of usage examples throughout the Detailed Description. This, too, is acceptable, provided that no important examples are omitted.

At the very end of the Detailed Description, just before the claims, there is a boilerplate paragraph stating, in essence, that the embodiments explained in the Detailed Description are non-limiting, and that the invention includes also all other embodiments related to the subject of the patent that would be understood by a person skilled in the relevant technological art. Here is an example of a typical boilerplate expansion at the end of a Detailed Description:

> Although only some embodiments are described herein, many alternative embodiments, modifications and variations will be apparent to those skilled in the art. Accordingly, the written description intends to embrace all such alternatives, modifications and variations as fall within its spirit and broad scope.

Not every U.S. ICT patent has such boilerplate language, but the majority do,[30] and this language ends the Detailed Description.

8. Review entire application: The claims should be reviewed once more to identify the Key Claim Terms. It may be advisable to have a person other than the actual drafter conduct this review — that which is clear to the drafter after tens of hours of work may not be clear to a new reader seeing the draft for the first time. The patent is not written for the drafter but rather for readers. A review by fresh eyes may be recommended in particular for patents that are known to be important to the applicant, which is true, for example, of Apple's "slide to unlock" patent discussed in Chapter 4.

Whoever conducts the review should identify the KCTs, and insure that each KCT is fully and adequately explained in the patent, or that the term is so well understood in the

---

[30] It is my experience that U.S. patents that originate from a European patent filing typically do not have such an expansive boilerplate at the end of the Detailed Description. That is, some European-originated U.S. patents do have such language, but most do not, in my experience. Conversely, the clear majority of U.S.-originated U.S. patents do have such language.

industry that confusion cannot reasonably arise. The draft should also be reviewed to insure that none of the most common patent mistakes have been committed.[31]

CONCLUSION TO CHAPTER 1

Mistakes in patents arise from failure to properly execute the steps required to write the patent application. Some common problems in the drafting of a patent include:

(1) Confusion about Points of Novelty. An application cannot be well-written if the aspects that make the invention new are not clear to the drafter.

(2) Failure to plan the claims before writing them.

(3) Failure to identify the Key Claim Terms.[32]

---

[31] In the patent drafting model presented here, Step 4 and Step 8 require review and, if necessary, iteration of what has been drafted previously. Step 4 insures that the Key Claim Terms are identified and explained. If the KCTs have not been explained, then they will be explained in Step 4, or the claims may be rewritten such that a particular term is eliminated from the claims. In Step 8, the entire application is reviewed for clarity and comprehensiveness. In addition, the reviews of Step 4 and Step 8 seek out the most common mistakes. If such mistakes appear in the draft, the application will be redrafted to eliminate these common mistakes. In an ideal world, Steps 4 and 8 would not be needed, but the creatures who write applications are not ideal beings, and so review and correction should be done. These steps are a kind of Quality Assurance for patent applications.

[32] Failure to explain an identified KCT is usually not the problem. If a specific term has been identified as demanding an explanation, in the great majority of cases the term is explained in some way. (The explanation might not be adequate, for various reasons, but almost always an attempt is made.) The more typical problem is that the word or phrase is not identified as a KCT, and so it is not explained at all. Terms that were not thought important may become important during patent prosecution or in patent litigation, but by then it is too late to explain the term in the written description. Truly, the identification and explanation of Key Claim Terms is one of the

(4) Confusion as to the purpose of a section.[33]

A good method for writing a patent will cover the invention, all its Points of Novelty, and all its embodiments. The method will identify all Key Claim Terms, and will insure that each KCT is explained adequately by one or more of the three techniques for explaining such terms. The drafting of ICT patents should be performed in three groups of sections, and in this specific order:

(1) Points of Novelty (possibly including a prior art search), claims, figures, and Key Claim Terms;
(2) The general sections Title, Field of Invention (optional), Summary, Abstract, and Background; and
(3) The Brief Description and the Detailed Description.

---

most difficult tasks of patent attorneys and agents, but also one of the most important tasks for achieving high quality and high value in patents.

[33] For example, the sole purpose of the Background is to set the stage for the rest of the written description, but never to include the invention. Each section of the patent has its own purpose.

Chapter 2

Principles of Litigation-Proof Patents

INTRODUCTION TO CHAPTER 2

Chapter 2 presents thirty principles for writing litigation-proof patents. These principles are organized by general topic, including (1) Characteristics of good claims; (2) Key Claim Terms; (3) Types of claims; (4) Patent value; (5) Seminal patents; and (6) Tips for writing patent applications.

Chapter 2 finishes with category (6) — tips for writing excellent patent applications. These tips are intended to form a bridge between Chapter 1, which concluded with a method for writing applications, and Chapter 3, which describes in detail the most common mistakes in drafting a patent application.

(1) CHARACTERISTICS OF GOOD PATENT CLAIMS

The scope of coverage of any patent is determined by the claims, which appear at the end of the patent. Each claim has three parts, which are (1) the preamble, (2) the transition (or "transitional phase"), and (3) the elements.

People often focus exclusively on the elements, in the belief that it is the elements alone that determine the quality of the claim. In fact, however, each part of a claim has its own function, and each part of the claim can add to or detract from the quality of the claim.

Principle 1: *A short and simple preamble is good.* A preamble such as "A telephone system" may seem too short, but in fact it introduces the topic, sets the stage for what follows, and avoids confusion.

Principle 2: *A small number of claim elements is usually good.* Each claim element adds another feature or dimension to the claim that must be implemented by an infringer. In other words, the more elements in the claim, the more features must be implemented, and the more likely that a potential infringer can slip away from liability. When people, including professional evaluators, evaluate an independent claim, one thing they do is count the number of elements in the claim — the more elements, the weaker the claim is likely to be.

Principle 3: *"General" elements in claims tend to be much better than "specific" elements.* A "general" element is an element that applies in many different implementations, and so might catch many infringers. Conversely, the more "specific" an element may be, the more likely that an infringer can avoid liability by either not implementing that specific element in an existing system or method, or by designing a product or service to avoid that specific element. For example, "communication system" is relatively general, therefore relatively inclusive. "Radio communication system" is less general, and so less inclusive. "Third generation radio communication system" is relatively specific, therefore even less inclusive than the other options, and thus less likely to catch potential infringers. This is not to say that a "specific" element is worthless, and indeed there are very many implementers of third generation radio systems, but the point is still clear that claims with specific elements are less likely to be infringed by potential infringers.

Principle 4: *A large number of elements might not narrow the claim if the elements are very general.* Sometimes a claim discusses a structure or an action in great detail, with many elements, and perhaps with many sub-elements to the specific claim elements. Usually this is extremely bad — the general rule is that a smaller number of elements is positive for claim scope, whereas a larger number will harm claim scope. However, a large number of claim elements may not be damaging to claim scope if the elements are so general that any person attempting the structure or method must fulfill the elements. For example, "A method for drinking water from a tap, comprising approaching a tap, opening the tap, placing a receptacle near the tap, collecting water in the receptacle, conveying the receptacle to a mouth, and drinking from the receptacle". Although there are six elements in this claim, all of the elements must necessarily be implemented by a person wishing to convey water from a tap to a receptacle for the purpose of drinking the water. Note that the claim does not cover drinking directly from the tap, or collecting water in one's hand and drinking from there (unless the phrase "the receptacle" is interpreted to include "one or more hands"). However, the claim does include all kinds of receptacles, such as cups, glasses, flower vases, pans, a balloon, and anything else that could be called "a receptacle". Further, the claim includes a situation where water is transferred to one receptacle, then placed in a refrigerator to be cooled, and then drunk — there is no requirement that collected water be consumed "immediately". Although much more could be said, the point is that despite the relatively high number of elements, the claim is still relatively broad, because the elements are all very general.

(2) KEY CLAIM TERMS

A Key Claim Term is a specific word or specific phrase that appears in the claims and that is very important to understand what the claims are about and/or the scope of the claims. A KCT may be clear on its face without any support, but if it is not clear on its face, then there must be some kind of explanation of the term in the written description. The failure to identify and explain clearly all the Key Claim Terms is the single most common mistake in patents, affecting without doubt the majority of ICT patents.

Principle 5: *Clarity of Key Claim Terms is of vital importance to the value of the patent.* Patent value is determined by the claims. The meaning of the claims, including their scope and their validity, is determined by the specific terms used in the claims. In every patent, some of the claim terms are "key" in the sense that they tell what the claim is or they avoid confusion. Words that might be unclear, or words that have multiple and conflicting meanings, must be explained. Examples of terms that may be confusing might include "software", "platform", and "virus". In one patent, the lack of an explanation for the word "interrupt" significantly harmed the potential scope of the patent.[34]

Principle 6: ***Patent litigations are almost always decided on the interpretation of one or a very small number of Key Claim Terms.*** Lawsuits of all kinds are often decided by one section of a document, or one paragraph, or one sentence. Patent litigation is even more severe than the general rule, because cases are frequently decided by a single phrase or even a single word. In one extreme case, $891 Million was paid out because of the interpretation of the single word "different" in one claim of one patent.[35] Comparative adjectives — such as "different", "similar", "same" — are almost always problematic unless they are clearly explained in the patent, but the general principle is not limited to comparative adjectives.

Principle 7: ***An attack by a defendant against a claim is very frequently an attack against a KCT, and such an attack can be defeated if the patent clearly explains the term.*** When a potential infringer tries to defend itself, it often says that it does not implement a particular element of the claim, and

---

[34] The patent is US 6,885,875, the specific claim is #25, and the specific element of claim #25 is element [4], which reads:

> "wherein the variable power adjustment increment is temporarily increased after the end of an interrupt of transmission between the first radio station and the second radio station."

Here, the word "interrupt", and the phrase "interrupt of transmission", are not defined or explained anywhere in the patent, and yet they are critical to understanding the innovation presented. For further discussion, see *TPV* at p.301.

[35] The Key Claim Term "different" appears in claim #1 of US 6,714,983, and it was extremely critical in litigation between Broadcom and Qualcomm, as discussed in *TPV* at p.177.

in particular, that the correct reading of a key term in the claim does not include the activity of the potential infringer. If the KCT is not clearly explained, this argument has power and may win for the defendant. Conversely, if the term was properly explained in the patent, the defendant probably will not raise the argument at all.

Principle 8: *However, if a claim term is very clear in the technology, then it does not need to be explained.* One patent discussed ways to "compress" speech signals, but did not include any definition of "compress" or "compression". That did not matter, because the concept of "compression" was clear and very well understood when the patent was filed.[36]

Principle 9: *The process of writing good Key Claim Terms is iterative — pick terms carefully, explain them, review the explanations, possibly add new terms with new explanations, rewrite all explanations, review the rewrites, etc.* Principle 9 may be the most important principle in this book, but it is unfortunately not always observed. Writing good KCTs is an iterative process. A first draft must be made, and it is important to pick the terms very carefully. Sometimes the initial round of selection and explanation of Key Claim Terms is considered to be the end of the task, but that is wrong, for two separate reasons:

First, the initial explanation of identified terms must be

---

[36] In US 5,414,796, each of the independent claims, method claim #1, apparatus claim #18, circuit claim #29, and method claim #48, uses the phrase "compression" or "compressing". In the electronics industry, "compression" does not mean "physical compression", but rather something akin to "short-hand communication". This is well understood in the industry. See *TPV* at pp.401–402.

reviewed, and then improved to the extent possible. Writing patent claims is a challenging task, and it is usually possible to improve the first draft. This reason should be obvious.

Second, despite the best efforts of patent drafters to identify all the KCTs, the first draft almost never identifies all such terms. In addition, in the process of drafting the application, new terms will come to the fore as "Key Claim Terms". It is essential that a draft be reviewed with a critical eye to identify terms that might be important to the claims, or that could be misconstrued and cause confusion. Which terms in the claims of the first draft seem to be important? Which terms could be misunderstood or wrongly interpreted? How are the claim terms explained in the written description? Are current explanation adequate, or must more be done?

After a review of a first draft, the Key Claim Terms will be identified, some KCTs will be accepted as they are, others will be rewritten, and others may be redefined or otherwise explained in the written description. It is essential to complete this process of identifying KCTs => explaining the terms in writing => reviewing the draft, at least twice, in order to produce good claims with clear Key Claim Terms.

Principle 10: *A Key Claim Term may be defined in any or all of three specific ways — (1) explicit definition of the term, (2) examples, and/or (3) an element in a figure plus accompanying explanation.* These are the three and only three ways to properly explain a Key Claim Term. (1) Definition is very explicit — "herein, the term X means _____". (2) Examples are good if at least two are given, and preferably more. Giving only one example is a bad idea, because the patent might be interpreted to be limited to that single example. (3) An explicit element in a figure, including an element number, together with the explanation of that element, is also acceptable, but make sure to state that this one illustration is "exemplary" only.

Principle 11: *Never use claim differentiation to explain Key Claim Terms.* There are three other ways to explain KCTs — use those ways exclusively. Claim differentiation is used by interpreters of claims, particularly courts, to understand a Key Claim Term that has not been defined, explained by examples, or illustrated in the patent. Claim differentiation is a doctrine of last resort, and should be used only by claim interpreters. When a patent drafter uses differentiation, the drafter can never be certain exactly how the Key Claim Term will be interpreted. If a claim term should be explained in the patent, define the term and/or provide multiple examples and/or illustrate the term in a figure.[37]

---

[37] An independent claim must always be broader in scope than another claim that is dependent on the independent claim. Therefore, if a KCT is used in a dependent claim, the broader independent claim will include that usage *plus something else*. What exactly is the "something else"? If the "something else" is defined, explained by example, or illustrated, then the scope of the KCT will be clear. If not, then there is no way to know in advance how a court will interpret the KCT. In my firm opinion, claim differentiation should never be used by the drafter of a patent application to explain a KCT, because the meaning to be attached to a specific term is simply unreliable. This of course does not mean that a patent drafter should avoid dependent claims with narrower scope than the independent claim. The creation of dependent claims is a common and accepted strategy to create backup claims against the chance that an independent claim is later invalidated. However, the patent drafter must never use these dependent claims to explain Key Claim Terms that are otherwise not explained in the patent. That is simply an abdication of control over the patent application. The improper use of claim differentiation is discussed in Chapter 3 as a common patent mistake.

(3) TYPES OF CLAIMS

There are different types of claims. Claims may be classified by the type of protection sought, including methods and structures of various types. Claims may also be classified according to the rules of patent drafting — there are independent and dependent claims, as well special forms for particular kinds of claims. The degree to which a patent has "claim diversity", also called "claim mix", can affect greatly the value of the patent. Generally, strong claim mix creates value in patent. Understanding "claim mix" requires a clear understanding of various types of claims.

Principle 12: *The most basic classification of protection is between structure claims and method claims.*

a. There are several kinds of structure claims, including, from relatively larger to relatively smaller, system claims, apparatus claims (also called "device" or "machine" claims), and component claims. There is basically one kind of method claim, which is easily identifiable by the "-ing" form of the claim elements, as in "identifying X", "doing Y", etc.

b. Every structure claim is composed solely of structure elements, and every method claim is composed solely of method elements. If a single claim includes both structure and method elements, that claim is invalid on its face. In this one sense, structure and method claims are opposites.[38]

c. The line between structure claims and method claims

---

[38] A method claim may include a step that is implemented by a particular kind of structure, but the implementation is still a step rather than a structure. An element in a structure claim may be intended or oriented or "configured" to implement a particular step, but the structure is still a structure rather than a step.

is often blurry. The particular type of a claim may be altered by changing the form of the claim. A single inventive concept, called here a "Point of Novelty" (or "PON" for short), may often be expressed as either a structure or a method. When a PON is intentionally protected by multiple types of claims, claim mix is achieved for that PON. If, in addition, the different independent claims share similar elements and similar claim language, the result is called "claim parallelism", which is one of the strongest techniques possible to provide maximum protection for a single Point of Novelty.

d. The most common way of converting a method claim to a structure claim is by the use of a "structural tag", which is a phrase that indicates a certain construct is ready to perform an act. For example, if one step in a method claim says, "processing raw data", this step may be converted into a structure element by saying, "a processor configured to process raw data", or the more general "a means for processing raw data".

e. Probably the most common structural tag is "configured to". Other common tags are "adapted to" and "constructed to". Although a patent may use any one of these tags, if the intent is simply to convert a method to a structure, then the patent should use the same single term consistently throughout the patent. The use of multiple tags in one patent creates a presumption that multiple meanings are intended, so if that is not the presumption, do not use multiple structural tags.[39]

---

[39] Claim #1 of US 6,714,983, uses three different structural tags, including "adapted for", "adapted to", and "arranged for". The use of structural tags is good, but the use of different structural tags in one patent is very bad because it creates confusion about the meaning of the claims.

Principle 13: *Good independent claims produce breadth of coverage. Good dependent claims produce depth of coverage.*

a. An "independent claim" is a claim that stands on its own — it is not dependent on any other claim in the patent. It is therefore the broadest type of claim in the patent, and defines the maximum possible breadth of coverage.

b. By definition, a dependent claim must be narrower than the independent claim on which the dependent claim is based. The reason is that the dependent claim includes all of the limitations of the independent claim, plus one or more additional limitations added by the dependent claim. Dependent claims back up independent claims. If an independent claim is invalidated by prior art, the dependent claim may still survive, since it includes an additional element that might not exist in prior art. In this manner, although independent claims determine the potential *breadth of coverage*, dependent claims determine the potential *depth of coverage*.

Principle 14: *There are special forms for specific kinds of claims.*

There are many special forms of claims, including these:

a. One special form is called the "means-plus-function format", which is a structure claim written not with specific structure, but rather with "means for" performing a certain action. For example, "means for processing raw data to produce information". In the U.S., the Supreme Court has determined that this format includes all of the specific structures described in the patent, but excludes structure that has not been described. This is considered to be a narrow form of structure claim.

b. A "Markush format" is a form in which an element in a structure claim is expressed as one of a group of things. For example, "a type of device selected from the group consisting of a mobile phone, a mobile computer, and an MP3 player". Although used originally for biochemical and pharmaceutical patents, Markush type claims are found also in ICT patents.

c. A "Jepson format" claim in the United States is called a "two-part form" in Europe. This is a form in which there is a lengthy preamble, followed by what the inventor considers to be the "improvement" in the elements of the preamble. This form is very rarely used in the United States, but is common in Europe. A Jepson format claim appearing in a U.S. patent is probably derived from an earlier European application.

(4) PATENT VALUE

Patent quality is one aspect of patent value. A patent of poor quality cannot realize its maximum potential value. Nevertheless, there are other aspects to patent value beyond patent quality, and even a patent of poor quality may have some value if these other aspects have been optimized. It is therefore important to understand the various aspects related to patent value.

Principle 15: *Claim mix adds greatly to the value of a patent.*

"Claim mix" is the degree to which different kinds of claims are used in a single patent. The mix may be method and structure claims, different kinds of structure claims, hardware and software claims, client-side claims and server-side claims, or other. It is generally positive to have at least some claim mix in a patent. Probably the most effective single protection for a single Point of Novelty in a single patent is to have a mix of claims protecting that single PON, in which all of the independent claims use the same Key Claim Terms and very similar language — this particular kind of claim mix is called "claim parallelism".

There are two advantages to having a good mix of claims in a single patent:

a. First, claim mix increases the potential scope of protection. A patent with a strong claim mix, particularly if the mix is centered on a single Point of Novelty, can cover many possible implementations of the PON, including structures of specific devices, organizations of systems, methods of creating or using the PON, and others. In one litigation, a court reviewed an early patent for digital video recorders, and found all the hardware claims non-infringed but all of the software claims infringed.[40]

b. Second, claim mix provides protection against the invalidation of some claims by the patent office, by an administrative body such as the International Trade Commission, or by a court. In one litigation involving US 5,623,600, all of the structure claims and some of the method claims were invalidated, but several of the method claims survived and much of the value of the patent was retained.[41] Similarly, in another

---

[40] The relevant patent is US 6,233,389, and the litigation is *TiVo, Inc. v. EchoStar Corp.*, reported at 516 F.3d 1290 (Fed. Cir. 2008), *cert. denied*, 129 S.Ct. 306 (2008). This litigation is discussed in *TPV* at pp.131–148.

[41] US 5,623,600, a patent about removal of computer viruses, was the subject of litigation between Trend Micro, Inc., and Fortinet, Inc., in both ITC Case 337-TA-510 and on reexamination at the U.S. Patent Office, Reexamination 90/011,022. This was a patent war with several rounds of litigation, but the

patent, US 5,414,796, it is likely that all of the structure claims, making up more than 60% of the total claims in the patent, are subject to invalidation, but all of the method claims would likely survive.[42]

Every patent evaluation, by any evaluator, must include, either explicitly or implicitly, exactly three general criteria. These general criteria are validity of the claims, scope of claim coverage, and discoverability (sometimes called "detectability") of infringement. The three general criteria may be abbreviated by the acronym "**VSD**", short for **V**alidity, **S**cope, and **D**iscoverability. Good claim mix will enhance both **V**alidity of claims and **S**cope of coverage.

Principle 16: *Five factors determine the value of a patent: (1) The market size of the main Points of Novelty; (2) The importance of the technical problem addressed by the patent; (3) The simplicity, clarity, and range of the technical solution to the problem; (4) The priority date of the patent; and (5) The quality of the patent.* (1) "Market size" means here both the total size of the market, and the number of players in the market. A market with many companies, each selling large volumes of goods or services, is a market with great potential. If a patent is infringed, the potential damages for

---

ultimate result was that the structure claims were invalidated while some of the method claims survived, and the surviving method claims allowed the patent holder to win a settlement. The story is discussed in *TPV* at pp.180–199.

[42] US 5,414,796 was never in litigation, to the best of my knowledge, and it is a patent that is very heavily cited in later patents, but most of the claims were subject to invalidation due to vertical shifting terminology within the independent claims. This patent is discussed in *TPV* at pp.382–404. See the Glossary, "Vertical Shift".

infringement will be significant. (2) Similarly, the importance of the technical problem bears directly on patent value. Compare, for example, a patent about the brakes of an automobile as opposed to a patent about the upholstery of the seats. Of course both items are important, but the patent about the brakes is likely to generate move value than the upholstery patent (assuming of course, equivalent filing dates and comparable quality between the two patents). (3) The technical solution must be simple and clear, such that infringement will be easily provable to a court. In addition, a patent claim that is "far-ranging", meaning that it covers the only practical solution to a technical problem or that the claim covers at least the best way to solve a technical problem, will prevent potential infringers from avoiding liability by designing around the patent. (4) A patent that is relatively early in comparison to other patents in the field is much less likely to be invalidated by prior art, and much more likely to have broader scope (since the patent did not compete with earlier patents). (5) Despite all of the foregoing factors, if the patent is of low-quality, meaning it suffers from many of the problems discussed in Chapter 3, the patent will not be able to realize its full potential value.

Principle 17: ***Value is created by both direct and indirect infringement.*** A "direct infringer" is an infringer who executes all of the elements of a patent claim. An "indirect infringer" is an infringer who "contributes" to another party's direct infringement or who "induces" another party to directly infringe. The market size covered by a patent includes all infringers, both direct and indirect, but in some cases, the indirect infringers may be even more important than the direct infringers.[43]

Principle 18: *Patents that are good (but not great) may also create value.* This principle corrects three common misperceptions.

First, it corrects a common misperception that the only inventions that matter are breakthrough inventions, that is, extremely major innovations in a field. There are very few such inventions. The vast majority of inventions are minor, but nevertheless important, improvements — for example, a structure or method for making a process speedier, or cheaper, or more effective. These are valuable inventions, even though they may not revolutionize a field.

Second, it corrects a common misperception that the only patent that matters is one that protects a breakthrough invention. This is clearly untrue. If the invention is not a breakthrough, but still valuable, then the corresponding patent may also be valuable. There are indeed patents that describe breakthroughs, but they tend to be as rare as the breakthroughs themselves. A very great amount of technical progress is not achieved through massive change and paradigm shifts, but rather in small and incremental improvements in the way things are done. These improvements are themselves valuable,

---

43 The topic of direct versus indirect infringement is discussed in many court decisions, the most recent being *Limelight Networks, Inc. v. Akamai Technologies, Inc.*, et. al, Case 12–786, 134 S.Ct. 2111 (June 2, 2014), in which the Supreme Court rejected an expansion of the scope of indirect liability. Despite this rejection, the total size of a market covered by a patent claim will still include both the market of direct infringers and those of indirect infringer. Indirect liability is an important aspect of patent value, and is discussed further in Chapter 3, Common Mistake 7 — Improper Mix of Elements Within a Claim.

and they are protected by patents which also have value. Only a tiny minority of patents have great value[44], but the mass of patents covering small improvements also add value. However, if the patent is not "good", meaning that it has many mistakes and fails to capture the invention, then no value can be created. Even a moderate invention can be well protected only by a good patent.

Third, it corrects a common and erroneous opinion sometimes expressed by managers of patent portfolios, that "we must do everything possible to insure we have the highest possible quality in all our patents". There are not enough resources to do such a thing, and honestly it is not worth doing. Yes, there are some patents that are understood, even in the drafting stage, to create significant value, and for these patents it may be worthwhile to invest significant resources in writing, reviewing, and rewriting the patents to cover every possible permutation and implementation. For example, that would seem to be the case with Apple's "slide to unlock" patent, discussed in Chapter 4. Most patents, however, are not in this category, and should receive only moderate investments of time and money. *Nevertheless, whether the applicant decides to invest massive or only moderate resources in a patent, it is my opinion that every patent should be "scrubbed" to insure*

---

[44] In most patent portfolios, and certainly in patent portfolios totaling hundreds to thousands of patents and applications, the bulk of the value is created by a very few "high-value" patents. In my book *PATENT PORTFOLIOS: Quality, Creation, and Cost*, evidence is presented that about 1–2% of the patents in a portfolio may be expected to be "high-value". The current book is not about portfolios, which will not be discussed further, except to note that the overall quality and value of a portfolio can certainly be enhanced if the owner insures that the patents are free of the common mistakes discussed here.

that it has none of the common mistakes discussed in Chapter 3 of this book.

Principle 19: **The potential value of a patent may be unlocked in a variety of ways.** There are several ways to realize the potential value of a patent. Some of these are (1) licensing-out the patent for royalties; (2) selling the patent; (3) litigating for infringement damages; (4) placing the patent in a "patent pool" to capture a portion of the pool's revenues;[45] (5) preventing competitors from copying the technology in the patent; (6) deterring competitors from initiating lawsuits by threatening with counter-suit; and (7) trading technology rights with other holders of patents or technical know-how. All of these ways of realizing value depend upon the quality of the patent, and in all cases the commission of the common mistakes discussed here can reduce or completely destroy the value of the patent.

Principle 20: **Patent value should not change whether the patent is acquired for offensive or defensive purposes.** "Offensive value" in patents is primarily the ability to extract benefits from the patent, as reflected in value groups (1) — (5) in Principle 19 above. "Defensive value" is the ability to convince other people to leave you alone, as reflected in value groups (6) and (7) in Principle 19 above. All five of the factors

---

[45] Placement of a patent in a successful patent pool is an excellent way to generate money for the owner of the patent. Patent pools are an important option for unlocking potential value in patents, and they are discussed at length in my prior book, *TECHNOLOGY PATENT LICENSING: An International Reference on 21st Century Patent Licensing, Patent Pools and Patent Platforms*, (Aspatore Books, a division of Thomson Reuters, Boston, MA, 2004).

that determine patent value, listed in Principle 16, apply to both "offensive value" and "defensive value", and in that sense, patent value should not change whether a company intends to use a patent offensively or defensively.

Principle 21: *The party most likely to be able to realize the potential value of a patent is a party expert in the technology of the patent.* Perhaps this principle appears too obvious to state. Indeed, most patents are created by people who are expert in the technology of the patent. It does happen, however, that a person not expert in the technology happens to invent something outside of his or her area of expertise. The full value of a patent is not likely to be unlocked by a non-expert.[46] Rather, the non-expert inventor should either sell the patent to a party expert in the field, or at least work with such an expert who is most likely to understand who uses the technology, where, and for what purposes.[47]

---

[46] Chapter 4 includes a discussion of a frequency hopping patent by the actress Hedy Lamarr and the composer George Antheil. These inventors were certainly not experts in the subject matter of the patent, and whether or not the patent is "high-quality" or "litigation-proof", no money was ever realized on the patent.

[47] The changing ownership of a U.S. patent is often recorded in the publicly available "assignment database" of the U.S. PTO, available at http://assignments.uspto.gov/assignments/q?db=pat. That database showed, for example, that US 5,606,609, entitled "Electronic Document Verification System and Method", which is about verification of electronic documents, was owned first by a manufacturer of set top boxes for cable television, then by a defense contractor, and finally by Silanis Technology, a company specializing in signatures embedded in electronic documents. A chain of ownership that includes multiple companies not related to the technology of the patent is uncommon, but it does happen.

(5) SEMINAL PATENTS

As explained in Principle 18 above, many patents are "good" but not "great". In contrast, "seminal patents" are patents that truly are "great". Seminal patents are those that document and protect major changes. Such changes are sometimes the foundations of new industries. Seminal patents for new industries are the "home runs" that people hope to achieve. It is important to understand some principles specifically for this particular group of patents.

Principle 22: *A "seminal patent" (1) has broad market coverage; (2) addresses an important technical problem or issue; (3) provides a technical solution that is an important innovation and perhaps the basis of an entire technical industry; (4) has an early priority date; and (5) has very strong forward non-self citations, or other clear evidence of significant value such as significant licensing royalties, victory in litigation, sale for a significant sum, or placement in a successful patent pool.*[48]

---

[48] This is my definition of the term "seminal patent". See also my prior book, *TPV*, at pp.66–70 and 305–319. To the best of my knowledge, there is no accepted industry definition of the term "seminal patent". Other parties refer to the number of forward citations as an important factor. See, e.g., Pantros IP, *Patent Factor Reports*, (2013), stating that the number of forward citations is related to both "patent value" (p.6) and "technical sophistication" (p.11); Joe Hadzima, *Patent Due Diligence: Strategic Patents & Acquired Liability in M&A*, (IPVision, 2014), calling seminal patents "highly cited patents [that] are more likely to be valuable and strategic than lesser cited patents"; and iRunway, *Patent & Landscape Analysis of 4G — LTE Technology* (2012), calling seminal patents "strong patents", and listing "forward references" as one of twenty-two parameters of seminal patents, pp.8–9. The industry appears to accept that strong forward citations are one indication of possible value in a patent, but as noted, I am not ware of any accepted formal definition of the term "seminal patent".

As stated in Principle 16 above, five factors determine the value of a patent. The first four of those factors — market, technical problem, technical solution, and priority date — apply also to "seminal patents". That is, a "seminal patent" will cover a large market and important technical issue, with a clear and important technical solution. It will have a relatively early priority date, which is an important advantage over competing patents.

A major difference between an ordinary patent (even a "high-quality" ordinary patent) and a seminal patent, is that the seminal patent has received some recognition from outside parties (*not* solely from the owner of the patent) that it is an important patent. Of course, a patent that meets the first four criteria and that in addition (1) generates millions of dollars in licensing fees, or (2) is victorious in patent litigation, or (3) has been sold in the past for a significant sum, or (4) has been judged "essential" to a technology and placed in a successful patent pool for that technology, is a patent that is probably "seminal". In addition to these four indications, however, one sure sign of market interest is that other companies cite the patent in their own later-issued patents. Many patents receive 10 or fewer forward citations from other companies[49], but there are some patents that have received 200, 300, or in rare cases over 1,000 forward citations from other companies. The importance or quality of an invention is not identical to

---

[49] According to a report of the Brookings Institution entitled, *Patenting Prosperity: Invention and Economic Performance in the United States and its Metropolitan Areas*, (February, 2013), the average number of forward citations for U.S. patents is 9.8. (This study was based on patents filed within the period 1991–1995, and counted the number of forward citations within eight years of the date of issuance.) Patents with hundreds or thousands of forward citations are in a different category altogether.

the quality or value of a patent. Therefore, strong citation by later patents does not mean necessarily that the patent has significant financial value, and it certainly does not mean the patent is "high-quality" or even free of the common mistakes described here. However, strong forward citation does mean that there are companies in the market that are interested in the technology described in this patent.[50]

Principle 23: *The strength of a seminal patent cannot overcome major mistakes in the patent*. A "seminal patent" is one that is important to various players in an industry, but not necessarily a patent that is well-written, or that has "high quality", or that is financially valuable. Strong forward citation suggests potential value in the cited patent, but the appearance of common mistakes in a seminal patent can destroy the potential value inherent in the patent. In particular, Key

---

[50] Very many commentators connect "forward citations" to the value of the patent cited. I am not aware of any writing anywhere that says strong forward citation indicates "lack" of value, although a few commentators suggest that forward citations show primarily interest in the technology of the cited patent rather than in the claims of the patent, and hence such forward citations are only marginally correlated with value in the cited patent. Articles that accept forward citations as a mark of value but downplay the degree of value include (1) James E. Bessen, "The Value of U.S. Patents by Owner and Patent Characteristics", *Boston University School of Law Working Paper no. 06-46*, (2006), (2) Alfonso Gambardella, Paola Giuri, and Myriam Mariani, with the assistance of Serena Giovannoni, Alessandra Luzzi, Laura Magazzini, Luisa Martolini, and Marzia Romanelli "The Value of European Patents: Evidence from a Survey of European Inventors: Final Report of the PatVal EU Project", (2005), and (3) Alfonso Gambardella, Dietmar Harhoff, and Bart Verspagen, "The Value of European Patents", *European Management Review*, Vol. 5, pp.69-84, (2008). These three articles are like a cup of water compared to an ocean of writings that support a strong correlation between forward citations and market value. I will not cite the ocean of articles here, but this topic is discussed at length in Chapter 7 of *TPV*, particularly at pp.312-313, and at note 174 on p.313.

Claim Terms that are poorly explained, or not explained at all, can significantly reduce the value of the patent, even though the technology described continues to generate great interest from the industry.

Principle 24: *A seminal patent may cover only some implementations, but still be seminal.* A "seminal patent" may be the basis for an entire industry that is based upon a new and breakthrough technology. However, a seminal patent, meeting all of the requirements of such a patent, may also cover a technology that is of great interest to an industry, but that does not rise to the level of "breakthrough" or "paradigm shift". Such seminal patents are also valuable. One example of this kind of seminal patent is a patent with claims to only one of several possible solutions to a technical issue. It happens frequently that there multiple implementations available to solve a technical problem — for example, hardware implementations or software implementations — in which each implementation solves the problem but with its own advantages and disadvantages relative to the competing solutions. If a patent covers a particular solution used in the industry, that patent is of value, even though perhaps not everyone uses this particular solution.

(6) TIPS FOR WRITING PATENT APPLICATIONS

After reviewing the general principles above, it is fitting to conclude this chapter with tips for writing patents.

Principle 25: *The writing of patents must be a creative process.* Patent writing is not merely a process of describing a

Point of Novelty relayed by an inventor. There are very many choices which must be made in the process — Which claims to present (and which to forego)? Which Key Claim Terms to verbalize the claims? How to explain each Key Claim Term? Which figures to use? The process of drafting must describe the invention, but it must do much more. It will happen frequently, in a good process for drafting patents, that alternative approaches for drafting the claims and the written description may be tried and reviewed. Some approaches will be accepted, some rejected, some modified, some combined with other ideas, etc., until the best mix of claims and written description has been achieved. There is a great deal of creativity in the development of inventions, and that creativity must be matched by equal creativity in the writing of patents describing and claiming inventions.

Principle 26: *Put the specific parts of a patent only in correct sections of the patent.* No one would ever think of writing the claims in the section entitled "Background Technology". Why, then, do people sometimes place definitions of Key Claim Terms in the "Background" section? All statements related to the invention, and all embodiments of the invention, belong strictly and solely in the "Summary", "Brief Description of Figures", "Detailed Description", and "Claims". Everything related to prior art belongs strictly and solely in "Background Technology".

Principle 27: *Write the written description in a way that does not limit the scope of the invention embodiments.* This principle would seem to be obvious, but it is often violated. Do not use words or phrases that unnecessarily limit the scope of the written description. For example, to say "in this invention" can be interpreted to create a requirement for the invention. Better would be, "in some embodiments of the invention". As a second example, any statement such as, "it is important that", or "a critical feature is", is extremely dangerous, and should be avoided. Explanations of Key Claim Terms or of usages or of features should not use unnecessary or limiting language.

Principle 28: ***Be consistent in the use of terminology.*** This is another obvious principle, but it is frequently violated. There must be a one-to-one correlation between a Key Claim Term and the way that term is explained in the written description.

(1) A KCT cannot be used in two different ways in the claims. This causes the single term to describe two different concepts, which is impossibly confusing.

(2) A KCT cannot be explained in two different ways in the written description. These different explanations may contradict one another. Even if they do not contradict each other, no one will be able to understand which explanation in the written description applies to which usage of the term in the claims.

(3) There cannot be a contradiction between the usage of a Key Claim Term in the claims, and the way it is explained in the written description.

Regretfully, I have seen all of these prohibitions violated in various patents that might otherwise be considered "good" or "important" patents.

Principle 29: ***Claim parallelism requires parallel language.*** Principle 15 explains that protecting a single Point of

Novelty with multiple types of claims provides very strong protection for that PON. However, parallelism is lost, and protection is weakened significantly, when the different claims use different forms of terminology or entirely different Key Claim Terms. Changing terminology among parallel claims is called "horizontal shift" (or "horizontal shifting terminology"), and will destroy the attempt to maximize protection of a Point of Novelty.

Principle 30: ***Tying an invention to one technical standard is extremely dangerous.*** Numerous questions and problems arise when an invention is tied to a technical standard. Assume, for example, that a patent states that it is applicable to "CDMA systems". Would this apply only to the second generation of cellular technology, which is sometimes called "cdmaOne", but which might be called just "CDMA"? Does it apply to the third generation of cellular technology, which has two forms of CDMA that are called, respectively, "W-CDMA" and "CDMA2000"? Does it apply to all versions of CDMA, or only to the versions existing on the date the patent issues? If a particular system of a potential infringer does not include one or more features written into the technical standard, is that system covered by the patent? Would the answer to the prior question depend on whether the feature is written into the standard as "mandatory" rather than "optional"? Under any possible set of answers to the prior questions, it would seem that a patent limited to "CDMA systems" would not include GSM technology or any other system that is based entirely on time division rather than code division.

Frequently, the error is not as brutal as saying, "limited to technical standard XXX". For example, I have seen, "most particularly applicable to systems using technology YYY". I have also seen definitions using only one technology, where, say, all of the figures use a single kind of technical implementation. All of these formulations are limiting. Tying an invention to a single technology, whether done directly or by implication, is dangerous. If at all possible, do not restrict any part of a patent to one particular technology or technical standard.

CONCLUSION TO CHAPTER 2

Chapter 2 presents some of the most important principles for writing high-quality patent applications. If these principles are observed, the most common mistakes in patent drafting, explained in Chapter 3, will not be committed, and the ultimate result will be the drafting and acquisition of patents that are high-quality and as litigation-proof as they can possibly be.

Chapter 3

The Ten Most Common
Mistakes in Patents

INTRODUCTION TO CHAPTER 3

There are three sources of mistakes in patents. First, the draft of the patent. Second, changes or concessions made to the claims during prosecution. Third, external events that are not related to the drafting or prosecution, but which nevertheless degrade or destroy the patent.

Common mistakes 1–9 below refer to mistakes that appear on the face of the patent. These mistakes may have occurred in the original draft, or by changes in the prosecution process. Common mistake 10 — External Events that Destroy Patent Value, is not an error in the patent itself, but is included nevertheless because of its importance and for the sake of painting a complete portrait.

(1) THE MOST COMMON MISTAKE: UNCLEAR KEY CLAIM TERMS

I have not seen a report or statistics that list the most common mistakes in patents.[51] Nevertheless, my experience

---

[51] I am not aware of any statistical review of patent errors. It would be

tells me that there is one mistake in patents that occurs time and time again, a mistake that in my mind is clearly the most common quality problem on the face of patents. That mistake is the failure of a patent to create a complete match between the use of key terms in the claims and the explanation of such terms in the written description and figures.

How common is the problem of unclear KCTs? Again, I have no statistics, but my experience suggests that the crushing majority of patents suffer from this problem, perhaps not 100%, but surely a percentage well in the middle to upper nineties in percentage of all patents.[52]

Let's think about what that means. People complain frequently about the poor quality of various products — for example, the much maligned "used car". A car purchased second or third hand can indeed have problems, but the reality is that most used cars run more or less the way they should. What can we say about an industry in which close to 100% of the products have a serious quality problem that detracts from the value and usefulness of the product? That is a description of the patent industry. It is most definitely

---

possible to review a random sample of patents, and on the basis of such review create statistical inferences about the most common mistakes. Such a sample would require definitions of mistakes, would need to classify patents by technology type (at a minimum, BCP versus ICT patents), and would need to track the age cohorts of patents in order to determine if types of mistakes have changed over time. The task would not be trivial, but nevertheless such a statistical review could be done.

[52] The patents discussed in this book are "ICT" patents, meaning information, communication, and medical device patents, but excluding the "BCP" Biotechnology, Chemical, and Pharmaceutical patents. Although I have heard anecdotal evidence about BCP patents, my background is in physics and communications, and I am reluctant to draw conclusions outside the realm of ICT.

not true that the existence of this problem in a particular patent necessarily destroys *all* value in the patent. Certainly that may happen,[53] but in most cases the patent will still have some value despite the unclarity in both meaning and scope introduced by this common mistake.

There are several different forms of mismatch between key terms in claims and in the explanation of such terms in the written description and figures:

(1) *No Explanation*: A KCT appears in the claims, but is not explained anywhere in the patent. If the KCT is unclear, the result is that readers, including a court, must guess the meaning of the term to determine both the validity and scope of the claim.

Let's take one example. Whether a term is clear or not depends on the context in which the term is used. Is the term, "mobile telephone", clear or not clear? This term requires, on its face, an electronic device that is portable (rather than "mobile") and that is useful for two-way verbal communication. Is that what the applicant intends? Then perhaps there is no problem of clarity. But what if the applicant means, "a phone that is used in an automobile, truck, bus, or other motorized vehicle"? That is not the standard understanding of "mobile telephone", and so it would need to be explained in the patent.

Does the term "mobile telephone" include mobile

---

[53] "Catastrophic failure" is what happens when entire claim sets are invalidated. In extreme cases, the entire patent may be invalidated. Catastrophic failure can occur due to various forms of "shifting terminology", which is defined in the Glossary here. In most patents, however, a quality defect creates doubt about the validity or scope of various claims, but does not necessarily invalidate entire sets of claims.

computers or other mobile data units that are not used for verbal communication? That would seem not to be included in the term "mobile telephone", but if that is what the applicant means, then the patent must explain the term to include this usage. The point is that a term which seems to be clear might not be clear at all, depending on what the applicant wants to say.

Here is a second example of a KCT that is unclear by lack of explanation. As noted, any comparative adjective automatically creates a problem. To say "different", without an explanation, is sure to create a problem. How is it "different"? On which criterion or criteria? To what degree? With what effect? Using such an adjective in a claim, and not explaining it in the written description, is certain to create confusion.

(2) *Conflicting Explanations*: There are multiple possible conflicts for explanations of key terms, including:

a. A KCT is used in one way in a claim, but in a different way in a second claim. This situation is simply chaos. It is impossible to know how a court will interpret the claims.

b. A KCT is explained in two ways in the written description, but these two explanations conflict. For every place where the term appears in the claims, does this appearance take on explanation #1? Or rather explanation #2? Or both explanations #1 and #2? Even assuming that these questions can be answered, do the answers create contradictions within the claims?

c. A KCT is explained only once in the written description, but the explanation in the written description contradicts the way the term is used in the claim. This situation is also impossibly difficult, and no one can know how the court will interpret the term in a specific case.

Every one of these conflicts actually occurs in patents. That may seem difficult to believe, but unfortunately contradictions are very common. They happen particularly where there is no explicit definition, but different examples are given in which the term is used in different ways. In one patent, for example, the question was whether the interface between an encoder and a decoder was by any electronic communication (a very broad term), or solely by compact disc (a narrower term) or solely in accordance with a technical standard known as CD-i (which as very narrow term).[54]

It is vital that the applicant try to create a one-to-one match between the explanation of each Key Claim Term in the written description and the way the term is used in the claims. Anything less will reduce the quality and value of the patent.

(3) *Non-Standard Explanation of the Term*: A KCT is used in the claims and the KCT has a relatively clear definition or understanding in the relevant industry, but the written description explains the term in a non-standard way.

For example, in one case, a company had patented a certain "metacode", and claimed that Microsoft's WORD program infringed this patent. In fact, however, there is a relatively clear industry meaning of the term "metacode", and Microsoft WORD meets some but not all of the criteria of that term. The company won the case, because in its written description the patent defines "metacode" in a much broader manner than the

---

[54] The patent is US 5,606,539, and the issue of the Key Claim Term in that patent is discussed in *TPV* at pp.270–274.

way the term is used in the industry. The general rule applied by the courts is that "a patent may define its own terms", and on that basis, the court applied the patent's definition rather than the industry definition. The company won.[55]

A good result for the company? Yes. A good patent? No. *Using standard terminology in a non-standard manner is certain to cause confusion.* The confusion here gave Microsoft a strong argument to escape liability, but there would have been no argument at all if the patentee had picked a different Key Claim Term other than "metacode". For example, the patentee could have invented a term such as "data controller" or "data interpreter", and then defined that term in the written description. *Instead of using a standard term in a non-standard way, create a new term and explain that term in the patent.*

(4) *Explaining a Key Claim Term with a Single Example*: As discussed, a KCT may be explained by (1) an explicit definition; (2) examples; and/or (3) an element in a figure with discussion. Although my personal preference is (1) definition, most patents do not have a "definitions section", and most patents define some but not all of the Key Claim Terms. Method (3) is excellent as a general summary of a term, but it cannot realistically include all possible embodiments, because that would require a separate figure for every possible embodiment — this is an option that simply is not within the realm of serious contemplation.

---

[55] The patent is US 5,787,449, and the case is *i4i Limited Partnership v. Microsoft Corporation*, 670 F.Supp.2d 568 (E.D.Tx. 2009), *affirmed* 589 F.3d 1246 (Fed. Cir. 2009), *withdrawn and superseded on rehearing*, 598 F.3d 831 (Fed. Cir. 2010), *affirmed* 131 S.Ct. 2238, Slip Opinion 10–290 (2011). The issue of "metacode" is discussed in *TPV* at pp.118–128.

I have seen patents where a Key Claim Term has been explained with no definition, no element in a figure, and only a single example rather than a list of multiple examples. Clearly the KCT includes the one example, but does it include anything else? Assume that a Key Claim Term is "fastener", and the only explanation is, "such as a magnetic link between the two pieces". Does "fastener" then include "a clip or other mechanical link"? Does it include a "hook and link connection" such as Velcro? Does it include glue or other adhesive? *If a term is explained by example, there must be multiple examples to expand the range of possibilities.*

(2) THE SECOND MOST COMMON MISTAKE: ROADS NOT TAKEN

In this case, the "roads not taken" are alternative embodiments, implementations, and usages that could have been described and claimed in the patent, but were not. One of the chief duties of the patent drafter is to try to think of all such alternatives, and capture them at least in the written description.[56] Unfortunately, this does not always happen. Why not?

1. It is often difficult to think of all the alternatives. A patent is in force for 20 years after the effective filing date. Who can conceive of all the embodiments 5, 10, or 15 years in the future?

2. There is miscommunication between the client and the patent attorney. In the real world, this occurs

---

[56] An embodiment that is captured in the written description may be claimed in the patent, or may be claimed in a later continuation of the patent. If, however, the embodiment is simply not explained in the patent, then the embodiment cannot be claimed at any time.

frequently. The client does not reveal an embodiment to the attorney, either by happenstance or by specific intent to withhold this embodiment from the world. Or the attorney does not understand what was communicated. Or the client insists that the patent be restricted solely to what the client is currently doing in its business — although such a focus may make sense for the business, it makes no sense for a patent, but this kind of thing occurs frequently.

3. A lack of resources prevents the full identification and description of all possible embodiments. In the real world, this, too, happens.

This mistake, which is very common, is not obvious, because unlike most of the other mistakes discussed here, this mistake is something that does not happen. It is a mistake by omission, similar perhaps to the exchange between Sherlock Holmes and Police Inspector Gregory of Scotland Yard in the story "Silver Blaze" (1892):

> Inspector Gregory: "Is there any other point to which you would wish to draw my attention?"
> Sherlock Holmes: "To the curious incident of the dog in the night-time."
> Gregory: "The dog did nothing in the night-time."
> Holmes: "That was the curious incident."

Events that have *not* occurred are often the most difficult to perceive, and that is true here as well. Embodiments that might have been presented but were not are simply lost opportunities.

(3) THE THIRD MOST COMMON MISTAKE: DEFECTIVE PARALLELISM

Parallelism, or "claim parallelism", is the protection of a single Point of Novelty with different types of structure and method claims, using parallel claim elements and parallel claim language. This technique, using multiple claim types for the same innovation, provides extremely strong protection for the innovation. There are three potential mistakes, however.

First, claim parallelism is simply not used in the patent. This becomes then another mistake by omission, similar to common mistake 2. The absence of parallelism is very common. That omission is not always a mistake. The creation of parallelism requires a conscious decision, and a commitment of both time and resources in writing the claims and paying the fees to file additional claims. The absence of parallelism can therefore be considered a mistake only for the most serious Points of Novelty, perhaps in seminal patents. These serious Points of Novelty are of such potential value that the company should do its best to maximize patent protection for these PONs, and therefore lack of multiple independent claims for these PONs could be a considered a mistake by omission.

Second, claim parallelism is attempted, but the claim language shifts between one claim and another such that parallelism is destroyed. The claims may still survive, but maximum protection is lost. I call changing language between parallel claims "horizontal shift" or "horizontal shifting terminology". Horizontal shift is a mistake that occurs occasionally. An example of horizontal shift appears in Table 3–1 below.

Third, claim parallelism is attempted, but language shifts

within a single claim, such that the meaning of the claim is unclear. I call this mistake "vertical shift" or "vertical shifting terminology". It appears rarely, but when it does, the results may be catastrophic, with both the infected claim and all its dependent claims invalidated for lack of clarity. An example of vertical shift appears in Table 3–2 below.

Here is an example of horizontal shift destroying parallelism, from US 5,414,796. In this patent, two aspects of one acoustical signal are processed, with different processing for digitized speech as opposed to digitized background noise. There are three independent claims, method claim #1, apparatus claim #18, and circuit claim #29, all of them protecting a single Point of Novelty — a type of data compression. Although the shift occurs at multiple points throughout the claims, presentation of the claim preambles will illustrate the shift.

Table 3–1: Independent Claims #1, #18, and #29 in US 5,414,796 — Horizontal Shift

Preamble of Independent Method Claim #1	Preamble of Independent Apparatus Claim #18	Preamble of Independent Circuit Claim #29
1. A method of speech signal compression, by variable rate coding of frames of digitized speech samples, comprising the steps of:	18. An apparatus for compressing an acoustical signal into variable rate data comprising:	29. A circuit for compressing an acoustical signal into variable rate data comprising:

All of these claims, in both the preambles and in the claim elements, focus on the same Point of Novelty, which is variable rate data compression. This is a perfect example of what should have been "claim parallelism". However, note the horizontal shift in terminology. Whereas claim #1 speaks of "speech compression" and "digitized speech", claims #18 and #29 speak of "acoustical signal compression". "Speech" and "acoustics" are not at all the same thing, and in fact speech is only one of several kinds of "acoustical signals". By this horizontal change in terminology, parallelism is lost, and maximum protection is not achieved.

This same patent, US 5,414,796, also provides an excellent example of the problem of "vertical shift". This mistake does not occur in claim #1, but does occur in both claim #18 and claim #29. In Table 3–2 below I have highlighted in boldface the specific words that cause the shift.

Table 3–2: Claims #1, #18, and #29 in US 5,414,796 — Vertical Shift

	Independent Method Claim #1	Independent Apparatus Claim #18	Independent Circuit Claim #29
Preamble	1. A method of speech signal compression, by variable rate coding of frames of **digitized speech samples**, comprising the steps of:	18. An apparatus for compressing an **acoustical signal** into variable rate data comprising:	29. A circuit for compressing an **acoustical signal** into variable rate data comprising:

	Independent Method Claim #1	Independent Apparatus Claim #18	Independent Circuit Claim #29
Claim Element [1]	determining a level of speech activity for a frame of **digitized speech samples;**	means for determining a level of **audio activity** for an input frame of digitized samples of said **acoustical signal;**	a circuit for determining a level of **audio activity** for an input frame of digitized samples of said **acoustical signal;**
Claim Element [2]	selecting an encoding rate from a set of rates based upon said determined level of **speech activity** for said frame;	means for selecting an output data rate from a predetermined set of rates based upon said determined level of **audio activity** within said frame;	a circuit for selecting an output data rate from a predetermined set of rates based upon said determined level of **audio activity** within said frame;
Claim Element [3]	coding said frame according to a coding format of a set of coding formats for said selected rate wherein each rate has a corresponding different coding format and wherein each coding format provides for a different plurality of parameter signals representing **said digitized speech samples** in accordance with a speech model; and	means for coding said frame according to a coding format of a set of coding formats for said selected rate to provide a plurality of parameter signals wherein each rate has a corresponding different coding format with each coding format providing a different plurality of parameter signals representing **said digitized speech samples** in accordance with a speech model; and	a circuit for coding said frame according to a coding format of a set of coding formats for said selected rate to provide a plurality of parameter signals wherein each rate has a corresponding different coding format with each coding format providing a different plurality of parameter signals representing **said digitized speech samples** in accordance with a speech model; and

	Independent Method Claim #1	Independent Apparatus Claim #18	Independent Circuit Claim #29
Claim Element [4]	generating for said frame a data packet of said parameter signals.	means for providing for said frame a corresponding data packet at a data rate corresponding to said selected rate.	a circuit for providing for said frame a corresponding data packet at a data rate corresponding to said selected rate.

In claim #1, there is no shift — the sole subject is digitized speech. In both claim #18 and claim #29, vertical shift occurs in element [3]. In the preambles and elements [1] and [2] of these claims, the talk is of "audio activity" and "acoustical signals", but in element [3] there is a sudden shift to "said digitized speech samples". There are two problems.

First, there is no discussion of "speech sample" in the preambles of claims #18 and #29, or in elements [1] or [2]. Therefore, the phrase "said digitized speech samples" in these claims is meaningless. These claims cannot be understood, they are indefinite under 35 United States Code sec. 112(b), and they are therefore invalid.

Second, even if the word "said" were to be deleted from element [3] of claims #18 and #29, these claims would still be invalid due to vertical shift. The rest of the claims are focused on "audio activity" and "acoustical signals", but elements [3] discuss "digitized speech". Are these claims about audio activity, or digitized speech? The vertical shift renders the claims indefinite.

What is the result of vertical shift in this example? If this patent were to be involved in litigation, it is likely that claim

#18, and all the claims 19–28 dependent on #18, would be found invalid. Similarly, in litigation it is likely that claim #29, and all the claims 30–46 dependent on #29, would be found invalid. Claims #18 and #29 in this patent provide an example of catastrophic claim failure due to shifting vertical terminology. Vertical shift rarely occurs, but when it does, the results can be very negative.[57]

If you wish to maximize patent protection for a single Point of Novelty, strongly consider using claim parallelism, with multiple types of claims focused on the same PON. However, if you use claim parallelism, be consistent between different claims (thereby preventing horizontal shift and losing parallelism) and be consistent with terminology within each claim (thereby preventing vertical shift and avoiding the risk of catastrophic failure of claims).

(4) UNNECESSARY LIMITATION IN THE WRITTEN DESCRIPTION

This mistake is a catch-all category that includes every act or omission in the written description or the figures that can limit the scope of a claim, but that was not really necessary to explain the nature or scope of the claim. Although every description is potentially limiting, it is important to avoid *unnecessary* limitations.

Here is an example of an unnecessary limitation by commission. Some patents state that they are limited to "CDMA technology", or that the invention "is preferably applicable to CDMA" technology. This limitation might have been avoided

---

[57] US 5,414,796 is discussed in greater detail in *TPV* at pp.382–404.

if the written description had said, "CDMA, GSM, and all other air interface technologies", or simply "all air interfaces".

Another example of unnecessary limitation by commission is the great detail presented in the figures, supporting written descriptions, and claims of the Monopoly® patents, discussed in Chapter 4.

An example of an unnecessary limitation by omission is the case discussed in common mistake 1 above, in which a sole example is presented for the Key Claim Term "fastener. When a Key Claim Term is explained by example, presenting only one example is an unnecessary limitation in the written description — rather, multiple examples of the KCT must be presented in order to expand the scope of the term and include alternative embodiments.

Here is another example of the same type of unnecessary limitation by omission. Assume that a user interacts with a computer or telephone screen to move items form one place to another on the screen. The interaction is by physical contact between the user and screen, but the only example given is "by pressure of a finger or other human appendage". What about the electrical signal between a finger and the screen? What about an optical, infrared, radio, or other electro-magnetic connection between a finger and the screen? If a KCT is explained by example, the failure to present multiple examples is an omission that may limit the claim unnecessarily.

This mistake may occur in the presentation and discussion of patent figures. The figures chosen, and the specific elements in the figures, must be sufficient to explain the invention, but at the same time must not be so detailed as to limit the scope of the invention. Accordingly, mistake 4 occurring with regard to figures may be by commission or omission.

If an independent claim is not supported at all in any of the figures, the claim may be rejected either by the patent office or later by a court. For example, a means-plus-function claim must have specific structure to support the means, and this structure is typically illustrated in a figure. If structural support is not found at all, or the structural support is considered inadequate to perform the means, then the claim will fall.

There are many variations of common mistake 4. In truth, as fallible people we are not capable of imagining and thereby preventing every possible "unnecessary" limitation in a patent, but we should do the best we can.

(5) IMPROPER USE OF CLAIM DIFFERENTIATION

The three traditional methods of explaining Key Claim Terms are (1) explicit definition; (2) multiple examples; and (3) element in a figure plus discussion. In addition, there is a fourth method called "claim differentiation", which is used very extensively by the United States federal courts to interpret patent claims.[58] This is a judicially created doctrine which says that no two claims may say the same thing, so an independent claim will always be interpreted more broadly than its dependent claim.

Here is an example: "1. A hollow wooden chest, comprising a block of wood with an empty space in its center, and a wooden top, wherein the block of wood is connected to the

---

58 See, for example, Mark Lemley, "The Limits of Claim Differentiation", *Berkeley Technology Law Journal*, Volume 22, 1389–1401 (2007), where it is stated, "The doctrine of claim differentiation is the canon that has arguably had the most significant impact on claim construction" (p.1391). The doctrine is said to have been applied by the federal courts "hundreds of times" (p.1392).

wooden top by a connector." "2. The wooden chest of claim 1, wherein the connector comprises a screw". "3. The wooden chest of claim 2, wherein the screw is at least 1 inch long."

The independent claim is the wooden chest with a connector. The first dependent claim, claim #2, specifies that the connector is a screw. By the doctrine of claim differentiation, the connector in claim #1 must include one or more options that are not screws, because if a screw were the only connector in claim #1, then claim #1 would be exactly the same as claim #2, which is not allowed.

Claim #2, dependent on claim #1, and claim #3, dependent on claim #2, also illustrate the doctrine. Here, the screw of claim #2 must include at least one option that is less than 1 inch in length. That way, claim #2 and claim #3 will be different.

What exactly is the problem with using claim differentiation to define Key Claim Terms? The problem is that when a drafter uses differentiation for a particular term, he or she cannot know how the court will interpret that term. In essence, the drafter could have controlled the application, but decided instead to abdicate control to an outside party.

Here is an example of the abdication of control. In the claim set presented above, clearly the "connector" of claim #1 must include something in addition to a screw, but what exactly? Is glue a "connector"? Is adhesive tape a "connector"? If a string is threaded through holes in the block of wood and the wooden top, is the string a "connector"? If a nail is driven through the wooden top into the block of wood, is the nail a "connector"? Note that a nail driven through the wooden top would not allow the chest to be opened — is the nail still a "connector"? If there is a definition of "connector" in the written description, or if multiple examples of "connector" are listed in the written description, of if a "connector" is shown in a figure and explained, the answers to these questions may be clear. Otherwise, all that can be said is that claim #1 is broader than claim #2, and claim #1 will therefore include something other than "screws", but no one knows what that "something" will be until a court decides. The doctrine of claim differentiation, when it is unaccompanied by any further explanation in the written description, produces unclear scope of claims.

Is it good or bad that independent claims are vague under the doctrine of claim differentiation? In my opinion, this is extremely negative, because it leaves interpretation to the courts, and no one knows in advance how a court will rule. In essence, to rely on this doctrine *without any explanation in the written description or figures*, is an abdication of control, a roll of the dice, and this is a kind of gambling that is not suitable for drafters of patents, in my opinion.[59]

Despite the abdication of control, is there a valid reason for a drafter to use claim differentiation? According to at least one commentator, one valid purpose for patent drafters using this doctrine is to claim specific "choices" (meaning alternative embodiments) without having to draw them in separate figures.[60] This is correct, and I agree also with the implication

---

[59] Some attorneys disagree on this exact point. Specifically, some attorneys deliberately draft vague independent claims in the hope that the court will give a very expansive interpretation of the independent claims. This is called, by some commentators, "gaming the system". Lemley at pp.1395, 1400, and 1401. This attempt does not always succeed, Lemley at p.1400, but some attorneys apparently feel this effort should be made.

[60] Robert D. Fish, *Strategic Patenting*, (Trafford Publishing, Victoria, BC, Canada, 2007, at pp.130–131, on "Claim Differentiation". This is a very useful

that doing a separate drawing for every possible implementation is not realistic. However, the preferred approach, in my opinion, is to explain the KCT in the independent claim with a definition and/or multiple examples, *in addition to the patent figures.* That is, I agree with the argument regarding patent figures, but the other methods to explain KCTs should be used by the drafter to explain the term expansively.[61]

Apart from the avoidance of extra figures, is there another reason for a patent drafter to use claim differentiation? There is a concept in patent drafting called "nesting", in which a single Point of Novelty is claimed with a very broad independent claim followed by one or more narrower dependent claims. The intention of nesting is that the broad independent claim may catch more infringers with its greater scope, but is also vulnerable to invalidation at trial, while the dependent claims have narrower scope but are more likely to survive challenges to validity.[62]

To have one claim set — including a broad independent claim plus one or more narrower dependent claims — in order maximize both scope of claim coverage and validity of

---

book for patent professionals — patent attorneys, patent agents, patent managers, and directors of Intellectual Property.

[61]   I am not at all sure that Mr. Fish and I disagree. He says, also at p.130, "Note that claim differentiation only works with dependent claims". The suggestion seems to be that the doctrine can operate only if there is at least one dependent claim that narrows the independent claim, and by definition that is true. Beyond that, however, the comment appears to focus on the mechanics of claim differentiation, and does not express any opinion as to whether the KCT in the independent claim should be *explained in addition to the differentiation* created by the dependent claim. My opinion is that the KCT in the independent claim should always be explained, and nothing in the explanation about Claim Differentiation in *Strategic Patenting* negates that opinion.

[62]   Lemley, at pp. 1391, 1394, 1396, and n.25 on p.1396.

claims, is a legitimate argument for "nesting" type of drafting. Truly, broad claiming and strong validity are in conflict,[63] and the only solution is to write "nested" claims, with broad independent claims and narrower dependent claims. But there is nothing in the nesting strategy of claim drafting that requires or even recommends presenting Key Claim Terms with no definition, no examples, and no elements in figures. Such a presentation is, in my mind, never justified. Even with nesting, the Key Claim Terms in the claim set must be explained.

To draft patent claims in a nesting style, with a broad independent claim backed up by multiple dependent claims, is standard and proper. To use nesting as an excuse for relying on the doctrine of claim differentiation is inappropriate and bad practice, in my opinion. The use of the doctrine of claim differentiation should be left to courts in cases where an independent claim cannot be understood. Patent writers, however, should explain every Key Claim Term in the patent, and should never rely on the doctrine of claim differentiation. In my opinion, using claim differentiation to broaden claims is a serious and avoidable patent mistake.

(6) LACK OF CLAIM MIX

Claim mix is a very important feature of good patents. To have a good diversity of claims is to increase the overall scope

---

[63] In *TPV*, I stated that there is "inherent tension between claim scope and claim validity" (p.58), and I illustrated this in Chart 2-2 "Scope versus Validity" (p.59). This tension is inherent in every ICT patent, and although the tension cannot be resolved, it can be managed with "nesting" type of claim drafting.

of all the claims, and increase the chances that at least some of the claims will survive challenges to validity.[64] In other words, claim mix can strengthen the V (validity of claims) and S (scope of claims) in a VSD evaluation of a patent.[65]

There many kinds of mix, including method versus structure, hardware versus software, means-plus-function versus other structure claims, system structure versus product structure,[66] and traditional method claims versus business method claims. Any of these mixes can, in the right case, improve the validity and scope of the patent claims.

Claims are written for specific Points of Novelty. A great diversity of claims provides strong protection for a single PON.[67] If a patent applicant believes that a particular PON

---

[64] The relative immunity of claim mix to invalidation applies only to internal aspects of the patent. In contrast, if there are "external events that destroy patent value", which is common mistake 10, such events are likely to kill a majority or possibly all of the claims in a patent, even claims of different types.

[65] "VSD" is an acronym for "Validity, Scope of coverage, and Discoverability of infringement". Every evaluation of patent quality and every evaluation of the financial value of a patent will include these three criteria, either explicitly or implicitly. Every time a specific claim is written in the drafting process, and every time a claim is amended during prosecution, the patent attorney should consider what may ultimately be the Validity of the patent (valid or invalid), the Scope of the claims (broad or narrow, deep or shallow), and the ability to Discover infringement.

[66] There are different levels of structure. The most narrow is component, or perhaps sub-assembly. The next is often called "apparatus", but is also called "device" or "product" or "machine". The broadest structure claims are "system" claims, sometimes called "network" claims. It is not true that broader structure claims are necessarily better than narrower structure claims, but rather a mix of structure claims increases the value of a patent.

[67] Strong claim mix provides strong protection. A special case of claim mix occurs when the diverse independent claims use parallel language in their preambles and claim elements. This is "claim parallelism", and in fact,

is relatively important, then claim mix — different structure and method claims — should be written for that single PON.

Sometimes applicants believe that their invention "is entirely a method", or "is just a particular structure". Therefore, according to this believe, claim mix is not possible for this invention. Or an applicant may feel, "I have two Points of Novelty, but one PON is entirely a structure and the other is entirely a method, so I cannot use claim mix for each PON." This thinking is simply incorrect. In the overwhelming majority of cases, a PON may initially be expressed in a particular mode (that is, as a method or as a kind of structure), but with correct claim language the form of a claim may be converted. For example, structural tags may be used to convert a method into a structure, or a structure claim may be converted to a method claim by focusing on the function of each component rather than on its structure. In practically all cases, a claim mix may be applied for a particular PON.

Should that be done? In some cases, yes, there should be a claim mix for a particular PON. In other cases, no, a claim mix should not be created. Why not? Because a claim mix is relatively expensive to write, may be relatively expensive to prosecute, and may cost more in filing fees. Patent writing requires that choices be made, and choice should be made such that some PONs receive much greater attention and investment than other PONs. Here is the tradeoff:

---

claim parallelism is simply one type of "claim mix". For a single PON, there is no stronger protection than the specific kind of claim mix called "claim parallelism".

Table 3-3: Options Involving Claim Mix

OPTION	ADVANTAGE(S)	DISADVANTAGE(S)
No claim mix	(1) Easier and cheaper to write claims. (2) Possibly lower filing fees.	(1) Does not maximize protection — both claim scope and claim validity are at risk.
Claim mix, but not claim parallelism.	(1) Greater validity of claims — the claims have greater resistance to invalidity challenges. (2) Greater scope of claims.	(1) More costly than writing with no claim mix. (2) Still does not achieve the maximum possible scope of claim coverage.
Claim parallelism	(1) The strongest possible protection for a single PON — all implementations covered.	(1) More costly than writing with no claim mix. (2) Limited to the single PON. (Other PONs must be covered by different claims.)

Despite the clear advantages of claim mix, in many patents it is not used for individual Points of Novelty. Some applicants prefer, for example, to write more independent claims for more Points of Novelty, and not to focus on a single PON. In some cases, resource constraints prevent the writing of many claims. If a considered opinion is made for whatever reasons to forego claim mix for a specific PON, then there was no error. An error occurs when nothing is done about this subject, and a claim mix is not written, solely because the mix was not contemplated. This is a failure of imagination, and it is a significant mistake in some ICT patents.

(7) IMPROPER MIX OF ELEMENTS WITHIN A CLAIM

Whereas lack of claim mix is an error of omission, the other mistake involving claim mix, which is improper implementation, is a mistake of commission. Although mixing claims in a patent is good, the mixing of client-side elements and server-side elements in a single claim is extremely bad. Why?

Mixing server-side and client-side elements in one claim renders the claim unenforceable due to the "doctrine of divided infringement". The general principle of patent infringement is that all of the elements of a claim must be carried out by one party. If this happens, the party carrying out the elements has committed "direct infringement".[68]

A second party might not carry out all the elements of the claim, but may participate, in some way, in the infringement of the first party. This participation by a second party in the infringement of a first party is called "indirect infringement" by the second party. Indirect infringement is a complicated topic, but broadly, there are two forms, which are "inducing" the first party to infringe (called "active inducement"),[69] and "contributing" a component of a structure claim that is infringed by the first party (called "contributory infringement").[70] There are three general requirements of indirect infringement, which are: (1) direct infringement by a first party; (2) participation in the first infringement by

---

68 Liability for direct infringement is created by the patent statute, 35 United States Code sec. 271(a).

69 35 United States Code sec. 271(b).

70 35 United States Code sec. 271(c).

a second party through inducement or contribution; and (3) intent by the second party to participate in the act of infringement.

In all cases, however, there must be direct infringement, which means that a single party has executed all the steps or all the structural elements of a single patent claim. A patent claim that splits the elements between two or more parties cannot be directly infringed by anyone, and since there cannot be direct infringement of the claim, therefore there cannot be indirect infringement of the claim. The claim is not invalid, rather it is valid but unenforceable (that is, no one can infringe it). Although the doctrine of divided infringement has been challenged several times in litigation, the Supreme Court has ruled, even as recently as June 2, 2014,[71] that the doctrine remains valid.

To include elements in a single claim that must be performed by two or more parties is a recipe for patent failure. The most common form in which this occurs, and it occurs quite frequently, is having client-side and server-side elements in the same claim. This is a serious and avoidable mistake in patent writing.

---

[71] In *Limelight Networks, Inc. v. Akamai Technologies, Inc., et. al*, Case No. 12–786, 134 S.Ct. 2111 (June 2, 2014), the Supreme Court decided that active inducement of infringement by a second party under 35 United States Code sec. 271(b) can occur only if a first party has directly infringed under 35 United States Code sec.271(a). This unanimous decision by the Supreme Court reversed a contrary ruling by the Federal Circuit, and essentially voided a $40 million jury verdict in favor of Akamai against Limelight Networks.

(8) IMPROPER USE OF NON-STANDARD TERMINOLOGY

We have discussed already the improper use of standard terminology in a non-standard way. An example was given of a well-known industry term, "metacode", used in a non-standard way.

There is another mistake, however, in which non-standard terminology is used in place of well-known and well-accepted standard terminology. This, also, is guaranteed to create confusion, and is a serious mistake. Here are two examples.

A patent claim has exactly three components, which are (1) the preamble (that is, the general subject), (2) the transition phrase, and (3) the body of the claim (that is, the claim elements). Assume a claim, "1. A table, comprising [1] a top and [2] at least four legs, [3] wherein the top is attached to each of the legs". In this claim, the preamble is "A table", the transition is "comprising" and the body of the claim is elements [1], [2], and [3].

There are exactly three standard transitions, which are "comprising", "consisting of", and "consisting essentially of".[72] The transition "comprising" means "what is in the claim, and potentially more". The transition "consisting of" means "what is in the claim, and nothing more". The transition "consisting essentially of" means "essentially what is in the claim, and perhaps non-critical additions as well". "Consisting of" and "consisting essentially of" are seen very frequently in BCP patents, but not in ICT patents.

---

[72] There are many more than three transitions, but the only standard transitions are these three, "comprising", "consisting of", and "consisting essentially of".

The only transition that should appear in an ICT patent is, "comprising".

The use of a transition such as "consisting of" or "consisting essentially of" in an ICT patent is a mistake, but this mistake is so egregious that it borders on professional malpractice, and it is very rarely seen. More commonly, patentees sometimes use a non-standard transition such as "including" or "containing" or "incorporating". Why would a patentee use such a non-standard patent term? The use of a non-standard transition adds nothing to the claim, but creates confusion as to what is covered in or excluded from the claim. In contrast, the standard transition term "comprising" provides the broadest possible coverage and does not create doubt. *There are many places to be creative in writing patents, but this is not one of them. Only the standard transition "comprising" should appear in ICT claims, and anything else is a mistake.*

A second example of using non-standard terminology when a standard term exists occurs in what I have called "structural tags". A structural tag is a term that expresses a state of being.[73] It is used to convert what would otherwise be the step of a method into a structure.[74] Probably the most common structural tags are "adapted to" and "configured to", followed by an action.

At least two errors are possible with structural tags:

---

73 The term "structural tag" is defined in the Glossary.

74 A claim can be either a structure claim or a method claim, meaning all the elements of the claim are structural, or all the elements are steps of a method. A claim that mixes a structural element with the step of a method is not permitted — such a combination would make the claim "indefinite", meaning the claim would not be allowed, or, if allowed in error, would be invalidated.

1. Where the patent uses a non-standard phrase, such as "set up to" or "designed to", or even worse, "intended to". These phrases are all unclear. Again, why use non-standard patent language, when there are two standard and accepted terms, either of which is completely acceptable? For structural tags, use either "adapted to" or "configured to".

2. Where the patent uses two or more structural tags. Here, one of the tags may be a non-standard term such as "intended to", which itself bad. However, it is wrong to use even the two acceptable terms, "adapted to" and "configured to", in a single patent. Shifting between different tags creates confusion, for absolutely no reason. Why did this shift occur? What does it mean? What was the patentee's intent in using two different terms?

Pick one of the standard terms, "configured to" or "adapted to", and use that exclusively as the structural tag in a single patent.[75]

(9) INCORRECT RELIANCE ON THE PREAMBLE

The preamble is the first of three components of a patent claim. Are possible limitations in a preamble included as part of a claim, or not? Quoted below is a statement from

---

[75] In claim #1 of US 6,714,983, there are three different structural tags, namely, "adapted to", "adapted for", and "arranged to". This single patent claim generated a massive win for Broadcom — a payout of $891 million. All of that money was endangered by the use of non-standard structural tags "adapted for" and "arranged to", and by the inexplicable shifting among three different structural tags in one claim. This apparently was a good claim, because it generated so much money, but the shifting among multiple structural tags was badly done and dangerous to the financial value of the claim.

the Federal Circuit Court explaining the rule for interpreting claim preambles. I have parsed[76] this quotation with numbers and brackets to ease reference to different concepts:

> In general, a claim preamble is limiting if [1] "it recites essential structure or steps, or if [2] it is necessary to give `life, meaning, and vitality' to the claim." *Id.* at 808 (quoting *Pitney Bowes, Inc. v. Hewlett-Packard Co.*, 182 F.3d 1298, 1305 (Fed.Cir.1999)). [3] However, if the body of the claim "describes a structurally complete invention such that deletion of the preamble phrase does not affect the structure or steps of the claimed invention," *id.* at 809, the preamble is generally not limiting [4] unless there is "clear reliance on the preamble during prosecution to distinguish the claimed invention from the prior art," *id.* at 808.[77] (Parsing in brackets [ ] added by me to ease the discussion below.)

So here is the test. A limitation in a preamble will apply to the rest of the claim if [1] the preamble states "essential" structure or steps, or if [2] the preamble "gives life, meaning, and vitality" to the claim, or if [4] the preamble is relied

---

[76] "Parsing" is a procedure by which a text is broken into its constituent parts for purpose of analysis. Patent professionals often do this with patent claims, but the process may be done for essentially any kind of text. In this particular case, a review of the Federal Circuit Court is parsed so that the review may be more easily analyzed and understood. See "Parsing" in the Glossary.

[77] *Intirtool, Ltd. v. Texar Corporation*, 369 F.3d 1289 (Fed. Cir. 2004), at p.1295. See also the Manual of Patent Examining Procedure, sometimes called colloquially "the U.S. patent examiner's bible", section 2111.02 "Effect of Preamble", available at http://www.bitlaw.com/source/mpep/2111_02.html (last viewed September 1, 2014). There is also a very good review in Fish's book, *Strategic Patenting*, at pp.77–84.

upon during prosecution to distinguish prior art. However, a limitation in the preamble will not apply to the rest of the claim if [3] the rest of the claim (not the preamble) describes a "structurally complete invention" and "deletion of the preamble" would not affect the rest of the claim.

In my opinion, the stated standard is impossible to apply on any realistic basis. Element [4] is clear to me, but the other elements are not. What is "essential structure"? What are "essential steps"? What is "life of the claim"? What is "vitality of the claim"? What is a "structurally complete invention"?

I am not criticizing this legal standard, because I recognize the very great difficulty in trying to interpret a patent claim where the intent of the claim is unclear on its face. I say only that on the basis of the law as stated, no one can possibly be sure whether or not a particular preamble will be read into the claim by a court, and if it is read into the claim, no one can be certain how the preamble will be applied to interpret the claim. In some cases, the preamble will not be read into the claim at all,[78] but in other cases, it may be read into the claim. In one well-known case, the addition of the preamble to the claim saved the claim and resulted in a $100 million dollar settlement for the patent owner,[79] but no one can be sure when or how that will happen.

---

[78] In the *Intirtool* decision, the court refused to apply the preamble to the rest of the claim.

[79] In *Uniloc USA, Inc. and Uniloc Singapore Private Ltd. v. Microsoft Corporation*, 632 F.3d 1292 (Fed. Cir. 2011), the entire preamble of claim #19 is "A remote registration station". Microsoft argued that claim #19 was a system that included both client-side elements and server-side elements, and was therefore unenforceable under the doctrine of divided infringement. The court ruled, specifically on the basis of the preamble, that claim #19 was not a system claim, but rather a product claim, and therefore the doctrine of divided infringement did not apply. Shortly after this decision, the parties

Using a preamble to save a claim is very similar to the use of claim differentiation to interpret a claim. These are both actions that can and should be taken by a court, when the court cannot otherwise understand what the claim says. But these actions cannot be controlled by drafters of patents, and should not be used in drafting or prosecuting patent applications. Reliance on the preamble is a mistake.[80]

It makes no sense to rely on claim preambles, because the patent drafter cannot be sure if or how they will be read into a claim. Short, simple, and unconditional preambles, with no limitations, are the preferred way to go in ICT patents.

(10) EXTERNAL EVENTS THAT DESTROY PATENT VALUE

In addition to these internal mistakes represented by common mistakes 1–9, there are also "external events that destroy patent value". These events, or mistakes, are "external" in the sense that they are not in the patent or the prosecution history. Rather, they are things that happened, or things that

---

settled the case, and Microsoft paid a sum reputed to be $100 million. This was an unusual case, and it does not subvert the rule that the patent drafter must not rely upon the preamble to inform the rest of the claim.

[80]   One possible exception to the rule that the preamble should not be used is what is known in the United States as a "Jepson format claim", also known in Europe as a "two-part claim". In this type of claim, there is a very long preamble, followed first, by a transition such as "wherein the improvement comprises", and second, by the body of the claim. In a Jepson format claim, everything in the preamble is considered to be an admission of prior art, and the body of the claim is interpreted as being an improvement on that prior art. This type of claim is common in Europe under section 43(1) of the European Patent Convention, but it is severely disfavored in the United States where patent practitioners do not wish to make any kind of admission of prior art.

were supposed to happen but did not, and these events (or non-events) harm both the quality and the value of the patent. Several examples of these events will be listed and explained at the end of this discussion.

Characteristics of External Events that Destroy Patent Value:

There are certain characteristics of external events that make them different from internal factors, including:

1. External events cannot be known by any person looking at the patent or the prosecution history. Consequently, a person reading the public file cannot know of this problem. It might be possible to discover the external event through additional research, but the patent itself will not tell the story.

2. As a result of the unknown nature of the external events, the patent office does not know of the events, and may allow patent claims that should not have been allowed. Similarly, a reader of the patent seeking to buy, license-in, or design around the patent, will not know the true scope or validity of the patent claims, and may therefore act in an inappropriate manner (i.e., paying too much to buy the patent, or investing in unneeded design arounds to avoid infringement when in fact the claims are already invalid).

3. These events may never be discovered. If they are not discovered, then they do not impact the patent, ever. Even if they are discovered, discovery may occur years after the patent issues, probably as a result of litigation involving the patent, and the value of the patent was

not impacted during the years the external event was unknown.

4. If such an event is discovered, it is likely to have "catastrophic consequences" for some of the patent claims or for the entire patent. In this sense, "catastrophic consequences" means that an entire claim set is invalidated, including the independent claim of the claim set and all claims dependent on that independent claim. In some cases, the entire patent with all of its claims is invalidated. By contrast, "catastrophic consequences" are rarely seen from internal mistakes — yes, these consequences happen sometimes from internal mistakes, but infrequently, whereas such consequences are very common from external events. Why this difference? Because internal mistakes tend to impact only one claim, or only one Key Claim Term, or only one Point of Novelty. In contrast, "external events" often suggest that the entire patenting process for the particular patent was flawed. The following examples will make this clear.

Examples of External Events that Destroy Patent Value:

Here are some of the more common cases of external events that destroy patent value.

(1) Failing to tell the patent office about an important piece of prior art. In the United States, there is no duty to search prior art, but there is a duty to make known to the patent office prior art that is known by the applicant to be "relevant" to the allowability of claims. Sometimes it is not clear if a particular piece of prior art is "relevant", but if the applicant knows of

a piece of prior art, knows that the prior art is relevant, and deliberately fails to disclose it, these actions constitute fraud against the patent office. If these actions become known, the entire patent, with all of its claims, will become unenforceable against all parties.

(2) Deliberately listing the wrong inventors on the patent. This is another instance of fraud against the patent office, with the same catastrophic consequences. Honest mistakes made in good faith can be corrected, but not deliberate misleading. This event occurs, for example, when multiple inventors are fighting over ownership of the invention — an event that happens not infrequently in the business world.

(3) External events that have occurred before filing of the application. One example is the so-called "on-sale bar". If a product or service is sold that includes the Point of Novelty, the seller may lose the right to patent that PON.[81] The patent office cannot possibly know that there was such a sale, and will proceed to issue the patent as though the sale had never occurred.[82] Although the patent remains valid while the event

---

[81] In the U.S., there is a one-year grace period. That means that a product with the PON may be offered for sale, and the PON may still be patented, as long as the patent application is filed within one year of the sale. In the rest of the world, there is no grace period, so that absolute novelty is required, and therefore patent protection may be lost completely and permanently by sale of a product that includes the inventive concept.

[82] The application of the on-sale bar is exactly what happened in regard to US 5,774,670, one of the earliest patents covering Internet cookies. Although the patent itself was of exceptionally high quality, its financial value is probably zero, due solely to this external event of a sale prior to filing of the patent application. This external event was discovered during patent litigation, 15 years after the patent application was filed. The story of US 5,774,670 is presented in Chapter 5 of *TPV*.

is undiscovered, the patent is always subject to invalidation at any time.

(4) External events that have occurred after issuance of the patent. One example is the licensing of the patent to one or more major companies. This event does not affect the validity or scope of the claims, and therefore does not impact the quality of the patent. It does, however, impact negatively the residual value of the patent for licensing or sale.[83]

There are many other cases of external events that destroy patent value. These events can have catastrophic consequences, so it is incumbent upon patent owners to avoid these events if at all possible.[84]

---

[83] Realizing monetary value from a patent is not generally considered "an external event that destroys patent value", but we can change the facts a bit to make the situation clearer. It happens quite frequently that corporations fund external research — in particular, companies may fund research conducted at universities. A very common condition to such funding is that the university grant to the company a license to the technology developed and to all patents based on such technology. Of course, the company most likely to be interested in licensing-in the patent is specifically the company that funded the research, but that company has already received a license, and therefore cannot be approached by a subsequent purchaser of the patent. To make the point even clearer, assume that the funder of the research is not a sole company, but rather an association of multiple companies in an industry, and all members of the association will receive a license as a result of the funding. Funding of this nature can happen at any time — before the patent application is filed, while the application is pending, or even after issuance (presumably for additional research). In all cases, funding of research by a corporate sponsor will typically be conditioned on a license of patent rights to the sponsor, and this license will reduce the potential value of the patent to a potential purchaser.

[84] I would not say that licensing-out patent rights for money is an event that should be avoided, but I would most definitely say that licensing-out patents *cheaply* can be a very serious mistake. Below-market licensing to a licensee reduces the future licensing royalties that may be obtained from that

CONCLUSION TO CHAPTER 3

Many mistakes can arise in patents. Some are mistakes of omission, such as the failure to use claim parallelism to protect a single PON, or the failure to use claim mix in a patent. Others are mistakes of commission, such as the use of claim differentiation to define Key Claim Terms, or the mixing of client-side and server-side elements in one claim, or the use of non-standard patent terminology, or reliance on conditions appearing in claim preambles.

The most common mistake in patents, the mismatch between Key Claim Terms and the explanation of such KCTs, may be a mistake of omission or commission. As an omission, this mistake takes the form of key terms used in the claims that are not explained anywhere in the patent. As a commission, this mistake takes the form of key terms that are used one way in the claims but explained differently in the rest of the patent.

These are all examples of internal mistakes, not "external events" affecting patents. These internal mistakes infect the crushing majority of ICT patents, and damage both the quality and value of such patents. That is the bad news. The good news is that these mistakes are all within the control of the patent drafter. Once these common mistakes are recognized, patents may be written to avoid these common mistakes, which will help the applicant obtain high-quality patents that maximize the value of inventions.

Internal mistakes can have serious results, but tend, in most cases, to be limited to individual claims or individual

---

licensee, and it creates a benchmark by which other licensees may argue for a low royalty rate. Licensing is fine, but it must be done prudently.

Key Claim Terms. In contrast, external events that destroy patent value tend to have catastrophic consequences. Further, once such an external event has occurred, it is practically impossible to fix. For these reasons, special effort should be made to avoid any such external event that can destroy the value of the patent.

Chapter 4

Examples of Litigation-Proof Patents

INTRODUCTION TO CHAPTER 4

After the prior discussion of the fundamentals of patents and a method of drafting patents in Chapter 1, principles of drafting excellent patents in Chapter 2, and the most common patent mistakes in Chapter 3, Chapter 4 presents several examples of patents that illustrate the concept of "litigation-proof patents". To be exact, five patents are discussed.

However, these five patents are *not* all high-quality patents. Some of the patents are excellent, but others are not. These particular patents have been selected to conclude the book because all of these patents are inherently interesting in their subject matters, and because they illustrate both the concept of "litigation-proof patents" and how patents lose their value when they commit the most common mistakes in patent drafting.

The book concludes with Table 4–5, comparing the patents discussed in Chapter 4 against the most common patent mistakes.

❖ ❖ ❖

Beauty, Brains, and Patents in World War II: The Hedy Lamarr Patent

Introduction:

Hedy Lamarr was a beautiful Austrian actress, and also one of the first stars of the "talkie" film era. Some of her first movies, in the early 1930's, might be considered risqué by today's standards, and were surely scandalous at the time they were made. But beauty and acting are not her main claim to history. Her first husband was a major manufacturer of armaments in the period leading up to WWII — she accompanied him to meetings with scientists, and she apparently understood very well what was being discussed. Hedy Lamarr moved to the United States before the war, taking up residence in Hollywood, California, where she starred in more than a dozen movies during the war years.[85]

In 1941, she co-filed a patent application with George Antheil, a pianist and movie composer, which on August 11, 1942, became patent US 2,292,387, entitled "Secret Communication System". This is a patent about frequency-hopping electronic communication, and it is, at least to some degree, part of the foundation for modern communication systems such as Bluetooth, cordless telephones, GPS, ISM-band private systems, WiFi, W-LAN, and others. What is this patent about, and according to the lessons discussed here, is it a "litigation-proof" patent or not?

---

[85] Brief biographical sketch taken from the "Hedy Lamarr" entry in Wikipedia.

US 2,292,387:

The specific objective of this patent is to enable the targeted guidance of torpedoes against moving targets such as enemy ships. Prior to this patent, the problem with torpedo guidance was that enemy ships could discover control signals, and either jam the control signals or send misdirections to the torpedo.[86]

The basic idea is to synchronize a transmitter on the control ship and a receiver on the torpedo at the time the torpedo is fired from the control ship. Physical observation of the path of the torpedo and the path of the target ship, from either the control ship or an airplane, would allow the transmitter to send signals, received by the torpedo receiver, to move the torpedo either left rudder or right rudder, and thereby guide the torpedo to the target ship. Fig. 7 of US 2,292,387, showing the changing course of a torpedo, is attached below as part of Figure 4–1 of this book.

To prevent enemy "jamming" of the control signal, or enemy "misdirection" with wrong commands, the patent presents systems and methods for changing the transmission frequency according to a pre-defined scheme known only to the control ship and the torpedo. The jumping or "hopping" among the various frequencies is not known to the enemy, who therefore cannot jam or misdirect the signal. Indeed, although the enemy would certainly be monitoring the expected frequencies, there was a good chance that the enemy would not pick up on the relatively brief control transmissions in different frequencies. Hence, the enemy might be

---

86 US 2,292,387, at column 2, lines 11–16, left-hand side.

unaware of both the control transmissions and the approaching torpedo.

The control transmissions hop among 88 different frequencies, since that is the number of perforated rows in a player-piano, which apparently provided part of the inspiration for the invention.[87] Fig. 4 of US 2,292,387, showing the changing frequencies on the strip of a player piano, is attached below as part of Figure 4–1 of this book.

Figure 4–1: Fig. 7 and Fig. 4 from US 2,292,387

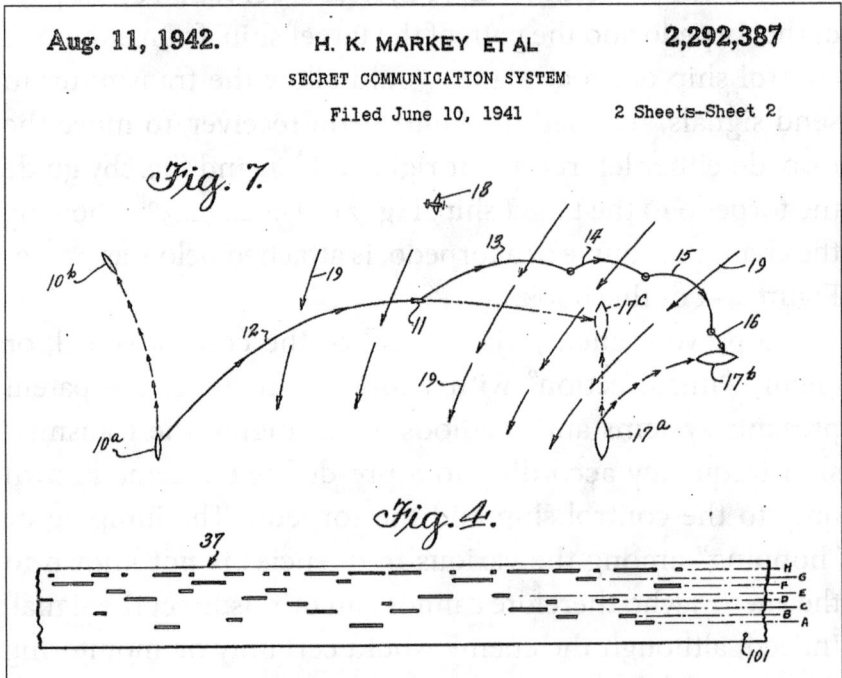

Aug. 11, 1942.   H. K. MARKEY ET AL   2,292,387

SECRET COMMUNICATION SYSTEM

Filed June 10, 1941   2 Sheets–Sheet 2

Fig. 7.

Fig. 4.

---

[87] The player piano and its 88 rows are specifically mentioned in US 2,292,387 at the beginning of the written description, column 1, lines 23–26, and again at almost the end of the written description, column 4, lines 38–40. The 88 rows of a player reflect the total number of 88 black and white keys on a full-size piano. The player piano was an important part of the inventive concept. The combination of frequency hopping radio transmissions, the

This patent was filed a few months before the attack on Pearl Harbor, and was issued by the U.S. Patent Office shortly after the Battle of Midway. The technology in this patent was hot, in fact so hot that the United States government did not permit publication when the patent issued.[88] Hedy Lamarr wanted to help the American war effort by joining the National Inventors Council, but she was advised by Charles F. Kettering, the legendary inventor and head of R&D at General Motors, that a movie star would do better to sell War Bonds.[89] The technology described in this patent was later used by the United States Navy in its blockade of Cuba during the 1962 Cuban Missile Crisis following the failure of the invasion at the Bay of Pigs.[90]

According to the lessons presented in this book, how good is US 2,292,387? Could we consider it a "litigation-proof" patent? To be brief:

— Despite some minor errors, the written description is, on balance, very good in describing the specific invention. It is surprising, perhaps even astounding, that a movie actress and a piano player were able to write a patent on such an important technology, but that in

---

perforated paper rolls of a player piano, and control of torpedoes, was an innovative combination of pre-existing elements. Although the combination is surprising, the use of pre-existing elements should not be. Every invention of every kind is only a recombination or modification of existing elements in new and surprising ways. Among humankind, there is no such thing as "creation from nothing" ("*creatio ex nihilo*"). That power belongs exclusively to a higher being.

[88] "Hedy Lamarr" in Wikipedia, third paragraph.

[89] "Hedy Lamarr" in Wikipedia, in the section entitled, "Frequency-hopping spread-spectrum invention".

[90] *Ibid.*

fact is what happened. This patent has many forward citations, and continues to be cited in 2014,[91] both of which facts reflect the importance of the technology discussed in US 2,292,387.

— The style of these claims from 1942 is much different than what we would see in patents today. Nevertheless, the basic ideas of this book still apply, and unfortunately, the claims in this patent are very poor, particularly in comparison to the outstanding technology presented in the technical description. The claims make almost all of the most common mistakes discussed in this book, including poorly defined KCTs, roads not taken, defective parallelism, unnecessary limitations in the written description, lack of claim mix, improper mix of elements within a claim, non-standard terminology, and incorrect reliance on the preamble.

On balance, this is a patent with a strong invention but weak claims. It is therefore not a "litigation-proof patent", but it does illustrate the principles of such a patent.

Written Description:

There is nothing like a "Background" section in this patent. The entire discussion of prior art appears not at the

---

[91] US 2,292,387 has been cited 51 times in the last ten years, including 9 forward citations in 2014 alone. The three most recent citations, US 8,771,184, US 8,786,495, and US 8,812,702, from July and August, 2014, describe, respectively, the use of frequency channel diversity to locate objects, wireless transmission of medical readings from a patient to a remotely located base station, and accessing remotely located computers while protecting data integrity and confidentiality.

beginning, but rather in two sentences at column 2, lines 9–16:

> "The remote control of the torpedo as described is old and broadly does not constitute part of our invention. However, it has been very difficult in the past to employ radio control of a torpedo, for the reason that the enemy could quickly discover the frequency of the control signals and block control of the torpedo by sending false signals of the same frequency."[92]

The first column, lines 1–53, left-hand side, is a very good summary section, although there are no section titles in this patent. The brief description of Figures 1–7 is adequate. The detailed description is unusual, in that the order of description is Figures 7, then 1, then 4, then 5, then 2, then 6, and finally 3. Despite this strange organization, there is no substantial difficulty in following the discussion. The following points about the written description are particularly strong:

(1) To begin the discussion with Figure 7 makes sense. That figure shows the method of operation by which a torpedo is directed to strike a moving ship. To explain the key objective helps the reader to grasp the entire invention immediately.

(2) Although the invention relies on physical observation to redirect the torpedo, the vantage point is not limited to the controlling ship, but rather may also be an airplane, which itself may direct the torpedo. This was a clever expansion when the application was filed in 1941.

---

92 US 2,292, 387, column 2, lines 9–16, left-hand side.

(3) Up to four signals may be sent and received simulta-
neously, but in addition there are three more transmitters which may send false signals to confuse the
enemy.[93] This is a nice addition.

(4) Flexibility and scope are added with alternatives.

— The specific number of channels, 88, is illustrative
only.

— The system could be engineered to control not
just one rudder, but two or more rudders (which
might be useful particularly for systems other than
torpedoes).

— The system described torpedoes in the water,
which would appear to be two-dimensional in that
the torpedo is near the water surface, but the written description specifically includes the control of
"aerial torpedoes" and "other types of craft in which
control in a vertical direction, as well as a horizontal direction, is desirable."[94] The term "aerial torpedo" is not defined, but the intent seems to be an
air to surface guided missile. Most particularly, the
expansion from "horizontal only" (meaning 2D)
to "horizontal and vertical" (meaning 3D) could
greatly expand the scope of the patent.

(5) There is no section in the patent resembling even
remotely the section I have called "definitions", and
which I have said should be at the start of the Detailed

---

93 US 2,292,387, column 3, lines 57–65, right-hand side. The language used
is not "transmitters", but rather "condensers", and presumably the concept
is variable capacitors.

94 US 2,292, 387, column 5, lines 11–15, right-hand side.

Description. However, there is a clear definition of one of the most important Key Claim Terms:

> "The expression 'carrier wave,' as used in the claims, is intended to define the unmodulated wave when phase or frequency modulation is employed."[95]

Despite these strengths, there are some deficiencies in the written description that also impacted the claims. Three common mistakes in the written description are common mistake 1 — Unclear Key Claim Terms (due to absent or defective explanation in the written description), common mistake 2 — Roads Not taken, and common mistake 4 — Unnecessarily Limitation in the Written Description. Here are examples of these common mistakes in the patent:

(1) Common Mistake 1: There is no explanation of some Key Claim Terms such as "control station" and "movable craft".

(2) Common Mistake 1: The role of human operators is not totally clear. For some reason, apparently simple negligence in the writing, a left turn is effected where "Key L is employed...", whereas, "If the operator desires to apply right rudder...he actuates the key R".[96] Is Key L automated, while Key R is actuated by humans? Such a difference between Key L and Key R does not make sense. Presumably both keys must be "actuated" by persons, although that is not what the patent says. The explanation in the written description is defective.

---

95   US 2,292,387, column 4, lines 22–25, right-hand side.
96   US 2,292,387, column 2, lines 41–55, left-hand side.

(3) Common Mistake 2: Many variations were not mentioned at all, and seem to have been excluded. Naval
and aerial observation of the torpedo are mentioned,
but why is land-based observation missing?

(4) Common Mistake 2: Why is the system solely one-
way, when a two-way system, which some kind of
transceiver at the torpedo, is clearly predictable?

(5) Common Mistake 4: An unfortunate phrase was used
that seems to limit the patent only to extremely brief
transmissions.

"A very important feature of system is that only relatively
few and relatively short signals need be transmitted... The
transmission of a very short impulse may not be discovered by the enemy at all."[97]

The phrase, "A very important feature", is unfortunate,
because it suggests that the system *must be restricted* to "few
and...short signals", which is a very severe limitation on the
scope of the invention. Yes, one could argue that the phrase,
"need be transmitted" provides brief transmissions only as one
option, but the scope of invention is now an argument, and
this limitation need not have been made at all. It would have
been possible to say, "In some embodiments of the system,
only few and brief signals are used, while in other embodiments, signals may be more frequent or longer in duration".

These examples of mistakes most definitely detract from
the presentation of the patent, but overall, the technology and
the invention are well explained, and I would say this is a

---

[97] US 2,292,387, column 4, lines 62–69, left-hand side.

reasonably good written description for the specific invention presented.

Claims:

The claims here, from 1941, are dramatically different in form that what would be seen in 21st century claims. Nevertheless, the principles of good claim writing applied in 1941 as they apply today. The fact is that the claims violate many of the principles of good patent drafting, and commit almost all of the internal mistakes most commonly seen in patents.

There are only two independent claims in this patent. They are duplicated below. I have added "T" for "transmitting station", "R" for "receiving station", "CS" for "control station", and "MC" for "movable craft":

Table 4–1: Independent Claims #1 and #4 in US 2,292,387

1. [Preamble]In a secret communication system, [T]a transmitting station including [T1] means for generating and transmitting carrier waves of a plurality of frequencies, [T2] a first elongated record strip having differently characterized, longitudinally disposed recordings thereon, [T3] record-actuated means selectively responsive to different ones of said recordings for determining the frequency of said carrier waves, [T4] means for moving said	4. [Preamble]In a system of the type described, including a control station and a movable craft to be controlled thereby, [CS] apparatus at said control station comprising [CS1] an oscillator and tuning means therefore, [CS2] a first elongated record strip having differently characterized, longitudinally disposed recordings thereon, [CS3] record-actuated means selectively responsive to different ones of said recordings for tuning said oscillator to predetermined frequencies, [CS4] means for moving said record strip past said record-actuated means

strip past said record-actuated means whereby the carrier wave frequency is changed from time to time in accordance with the recordings on said strip,

[R]a receiving station including

[R1] carrier wave-receiving means having tuning means tunable to said carrier wave frequencies,

[R2] a second record strip,

[R3] record-actuated means selectively responsive to different recordings on said second record strip for tuning said receiver to said predetermined carrier frequencies, and

[R4] means for moving said second strip past its associated record-actuated means in synchronism with said first strip, whereby

[T&R]the record-actuated means at the transmitting station and at the receiving station, respectively, are actuated in synchronism to maintain the receiver tuned to the carrier frequency of the transmitter.

[CS5] whereby the frequency of oscillation is changed from time to time in accordance with the recordings on said strip, and

[CS6] means for selectively transmitting radio signals corresponding in frequency to the said frequency of oscillation;

[MC] apparatus on said movable craft comprising

[MC1] a radio receiver having tuning means tunable to said predetermined frequencies,

[MC2] a second record strip,

[MC3] record-actuated means selectively responsive to different recordings on said second strip for tuning said receiver to said predetermined frequencies,

[MC4] means for moving said second strip past its associated record-actuated means in synchronism with said first strip whereby the record-actuated means at the control station and on the movable craft, respectively, are actuated in synchronism to maintain said radio receiver tuned to the frequency of oscillation of the transmitter;

[MC5] mechanism on said craft for selectively determining its movement, and

[MC6] means responsive to radio signals received by said receiver for controlling said mechanism.

We can start by observing that both of these claims are simply too long and too complicated to be of much value. There are times when relatively long claims are justified or even required, but the claims #1 and #4 in US 2,292,387 could have obtained the same results with less description and with shorter claims (by breaking each of claim #1 and claim #4 into shorter and simpler claims).

Claim #1 is 168 words — far too long. It has three elements and eight sub-elements, and these sub-elements are not so short or so general as to catch infringers. Claim #4 is 128 words — again, much too long. Claim #4 has two elements, and eleven long and complicated sub-elements which are probably not implemented by any infringer. Long claims, with long, complicated elements and sub-elements, are not likely to be infringed.

The entire preamble in claim #1 is, "In a secret communication system". Although claim #1 in general is too complicated, the preamble is excellent in its brevity and the clarity. The adjective "secret" in the preamble is superfluous, and would not be seen in today claims, but this adjective might not be interpreted by a court to limit the scope of the claim.[98] The preamble for claim #4 is, "In a system of the type described, including a control station and a movable craft to be controlled thereby". This preamble of claim #4 is too long, and the phrase "of the type described" would not be seen in modern patents.

In each claim, the preamble appears to be an integral part of the claim — that is to say, each claim seems to commit common mistake 9 — Incorrect Reliance on the Preamble. Further, each of the independent claims seems to be made up of two sub-claims. Each such sub-claim could have been its own independent claim — much shorter and simpler than

---

[98] A court may or may not apply words and phrases in a preamble to limit the scope of a claim. The court tries to determine the patentee's intent. Here, the court could well determine that the intent is not to limit the claim, but rather to indicate that the frequency hopping technology described here is, by its nature, "secret", meaning hard to detect or jam. Hence, the adjective "secret" is not limiting, but simply descriptive of what the technology is. In other words, the word does not limit the claims to "secret system", and thereby exclude "open" or "non-secret systems", but simply indicates that implementation of the technology will create communication that cannot be easily intercepted.

the original independent claims. Claim #1 seems to include a sub-claim for "transmitting station" and a sub-claim for "receiving station". These two sub-claims do not fit together, except in the context of the "secret communication system" of the preamble. Similarly, claim #4 is actually composed of two separate sub-claims, one for an "apparatus at a control station" and a second for an "apparatus on a movable craft". These sub-claims do not fit together, except in the context of the preamble "system of the type described" in the preamble.

For each independent claim, the transitional phrase, "including", is simply bad practice, that is, commission of common mistake 8 — Improper Use of Non-Standard Terminology. This was not merely the style of writing in 1941. In claim #4, each sub-claim correctly uses the standard term "comprising", at [CS] and [MC], respectively. The use of the transitional phase "comprising" in claim #4 proves that this standard terminology was known at the time of the patent. The transitional phrase, "including", is sometimes used in today's patents, but it is inferior to the well-known and well-accepted transition "comprising".[99]

The most common mistake in patents is the improper explanation of Key Claim Terms. Regarding this mistake, the patent has a mixed record. On the one hand, there are many elements which are not explained, but which probably do not require any explanation since they appear to be clear on their face. For example, "transmitting station", "plurality

---

[99] Use of a non-standard transition, such as "including", always creates a risk that the court will interpret a claim narrowly, to include only what is specifically written in the claim and excluding any possible additions. In today's Information & Communication Technologies patents, the only transition that should be seen is "comprising".

of frequencies", "receiving station", "tuning", "tunable", and "synchronism",[100] all seem to be standard industry terms. Also, as noted, the key term "carrier wave" is defined at column 4, lines 22–25, right-hand side.

However, some other terms are not explained, and are not so clear. I would note here, for example, "control station", which seems to be the same thing as "transmitting station" but which is not defined or explained. Is "control station" the same thing as "transmitting station"? If so, why are two Key Claim Terms used for a single concept? If not, then how is "control station" different from "transmitting station"? Similarly, the KCT "movable craft" appears to be synonymous with "receiving station", although there is no explanation so this is impossible to know for certain. Moreover, the entire patent is about controlling the direction of torpedoes, so apparently "movable craft" includes at least "torpedo", and possibly something else as well. Overall, a weak presentation of these Key Claim Terms, although, as indicated, some of the terms are very clear.

For the common mistake 2 — Roads Not Taken, the patent does well to include both naval and aerial control, but why did it not include land-based control? Also, the system appears to be one-way in all its embodiments, that is, from the controller to the torpedo. Why would two-way systems be excluded? There are some very nice additions in the patent, including multiple transmitters, multiple rudders, and others, but overall, the patent has a mixed record on common mistake 2.

Common mistake 3 — Defective Parallelism, is prominent in this patent, but in a unique form. There is not clear

---

[100] The term "synchronism" would more likely appear today as "synchronization", but the idea is the same.

parallelism between independent claims #1 and #4, but there is parallelism *within* each independent claim. The four elements of the transmitter in claim #1 parallel the four elements of the receiver in claim #1, but the language keeps shifting between these two sub-claims. As only one example, the receiver in claim #1 uses the phrase "tuning" four times ("tuning means" and "tunable" in R1, and "tuning" in R3), but this phrase does not appear at all in the transmitter of claim #1. As to claim #4, it seems likely that the drafter intended parallel treatment for the "control station apparatus" and the "movable craft apparatus", but there are so many changes in language that parallelism is simply not achieved.

There is very little claim mix in this patent. All the claims are for products — "transmitting station" and "receiving station" — or for components — "control station apparatus" and "movable craft apparatus". There are no system claims, despite the preambles of claim #1 and #4. There are no method claims at all, which is surprising given that the essence of the invention is to control the direction of a torpedo. In short, common mistake 6 — Lack of Claim Mix, is prevalent.[101]

---

[101] The absence of any system claims for what appears to be a system for controlling a torpedo is indeed surprising. However, the absence of method claims is surprising only from the modern viewpoint, but would have been expected when this patent was filed and issued in the early 1940's. The original patent law, embodied in the U.S. Patent Act of 1790, listed as patentable subjects, "any useful art, manufacture, engine, machine, or device, or any improvement therein..." (section 1 of the Patent Act of 1790). Despite subsequent changes in the statute, the patentable category "process" was added only by the U.S. Patent Act of 1952, at which time "art" as a category was replaced by "process" (35 United States Code sec. 101). Prior to the change in 1952, patents would include product claims, system claims, and claims to methods for manufacturing items, but would not include general processes or anything that might be considered a "business method". Thus, we might have seen in the 1940's "a method for manufacturing a system to control

Common mistake 7 — Improper Mix of Elements Within a Claim, also appears. The essence of this mistake is to include server-side and client-side elements in one claim, but that is exactly what is done in both claim #1 (the server-side "transmitting station" and the client-side "receiving station), and claim #4 (the server-side "control station apparatus" and the client-side "movable craft apparatus"). In this particular case, the split might not matter, because the entire system, both the controller and the torpedo, is operated by one entity. However, cases could easily be imagined where there is a split in operation between a controller and a controlled "movable craft". In general, this mistake appears very clearly in the patent, and it is bad practice. Why did the patent writer choose to write the claims in this way, instead of splitting claim #1 into two claims (transmitter and receiver) and #4 into two claims (control station and movable craft)? I do not know the answer.

Claim differentiation does not appear to have been used, so that mistake was not made. No external factors that destroy patent value are evident on the face of the patent. On balance, however, the claims are badly written and the patent is not strong.

CONCLUSION ABOUT THE HEDY LAMARR PATENT:

This patent was written by the beautiful film star Hedy

---

torpedoes", but we would not have seen in U.S. 2,292,387 or anywhere else, "a method for controlling the direction of a torpedo". From the modern perspective, the absence of any method claims in this patent weakens the claim mix, and in that sense may be considered a mistake, but of course it was not a mistake when the patent was written in 1941, since such method claims would not have been filed or allowed at that time.

Lamarr and the Hollywood composer George Antheil. The written description in the patent was good in 1941, and is good even by today's standards. The technology was used by the United States Navy in the 1960's, and it is one of the bases for some of today's most advanced mobile communication technologies.

Unfortunately, although the technology of the patent is very strong, the patent claims commit almost all of the most common mistakes found in the drafting of patent. As a result, the patent is weak overall, and does not adequately protect what was an invention that was truly outstanding in its time.

❖   ❖   ❖

Does a Patent Give a Monopoly on Monopoly®?

Introduction:

All kinds of games are patentable. Board games in particular are patentable. The game Monopoly® is possibly the most popular board of all time (after chess and checkers), and it has a patent covering it. Actually, there are three patents for the game of Monopoly®. How is it possible that there are three different patents for the same board game?

The first patent, filed in 1903 and granted in 1904, was issued to Lizzie J. Magie, who was, by all accounts a devout believer in the "single land tax", a system for funding all governmental activities through a single tax on the value of unimproved land. This system was created by David Ricardo, John Stuart Mill, and Henry George in the 19th century, and was very popular in its heyday. In order to illustrate this system, and to illustrate in particular the evils of monopoly over land, Magie invented a game she called "The Landlord's Game", and patented the game in US 748,626. The front page of that patent, with an illustration of the board, appears below as Figure 4–2.[102]

Lizzie Magie's first patent expired in 1921. She then filed a new application in 1923, granted in 1924, resulting in US 1,509,312. This second patent also covers "The Landlord's Game", but now there are specific street names from a variety of places, including New York City ("Broadway" and "the Bowery"), and Chicago ("Lake Shore Drive" and "the Loop"). The board includes also what I take to be humorous names ("Easy Street", "I.B. Sharpe Real Estate", and "Hell's Half Acre"). The front page of this second patent, with an illustration of this second patent, appears below as Figure 4–3.[103]

Finally, in 1935, Charles B. Darrow filed and received a patent for exactly the game we know today as Monopoly®. That patent is US 2,026,082, and the front page, with an illustration of the board, appears below as Figure 4–4.[104]

---

[102] A clearer view of the front page of US 748,626, may be seen at the database of the U.S. Patent Office, http://pdfpiw.uspto.gov/.piw?Docid=748626&idkey=NONE&homeurl=http%3A%252F%252Fpatft.uspto.gov%252Fneta html%252FPTO%252Fpatimg.htm, or through the freely accessible database freepatentsonline.com at http://www.freepatentsonline.com/0748626.pdf.

[103] A clearer view of the front page of US 1,509,312, may be seen at http://pdfpiw.uspto.gov/.piw?Docid=1509312&idkey=NONE&homeurl=http%3A%252F%252Fpatft.uspto.gov%252Fnetahtml%252FPTO%252Fpatimg.htm, or at http://www.freepatentsonline.com/1509312.pdf.

[104] A clearer view of the front page of US 2,026,082, may be seen at http://pdfpiw.uspto.gov/.piw?Docid=2026082&idkey=NONE&homeurl=http%3A%252F%252Fpatft.uspto.gov%252Fnetahtml%252FPTO%252Fpatimg.htm, or at http://www.freepatentsonline.com/2026082.pdf.

Figure 4-2: Front Page of US 748,626

No. 748,626. PATENTED JAN. 5, 1904.

L. J. MAGIE.

GAME BOARD.

APPLICATION FILED MAR. 23, 1903.

NO MODEL. 2 SHEETS—SHEET 1.

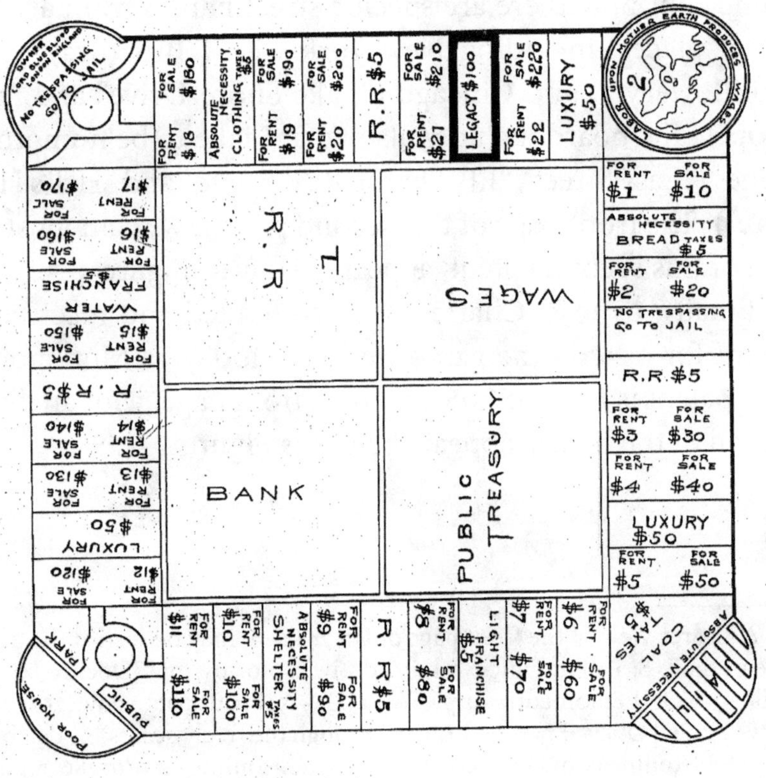

Fig. 1

Witnesses

F. L. Ourand

W. H. Ourand

Inventor

Lizzie J. Magie

by John A. Saul

Attorney

Figure 4–3: Front Page of US 1,509,312

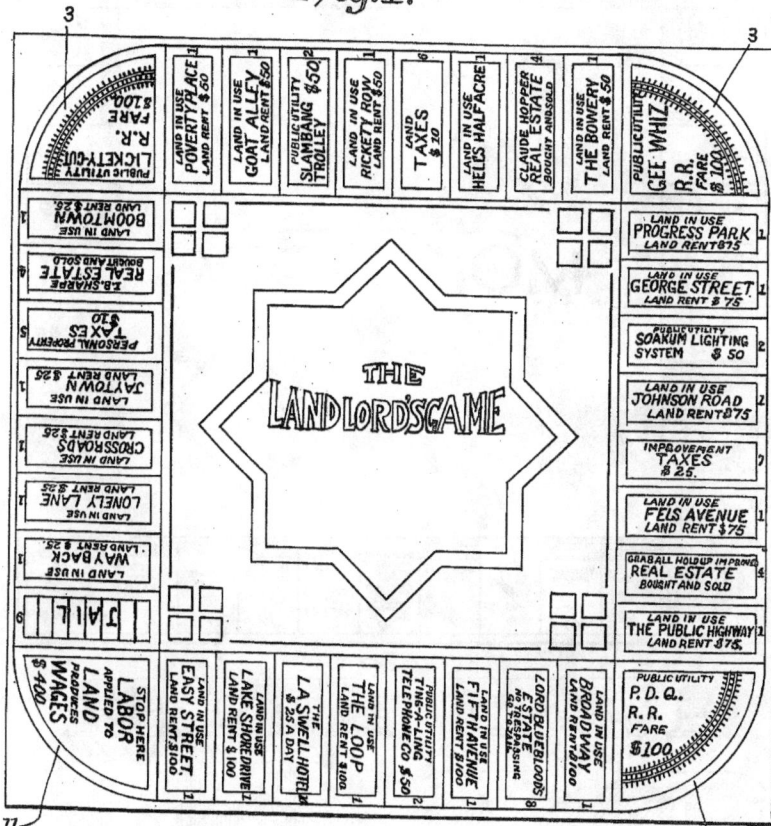

Sept. 23 , 1924.

E. M. PHILLIPS

GAME BOARD

Filed April 28 . 1923

1,509,312

2 Sheets—Sheet 1

Fig.1.

Figure 4–4: Front Page of US 2,206,082

Dec. 31, 1935.   C. B. DARROW   2,026,082

BOARD GAME APPARATUS

Filed Aug. 31, 1935   7 Sheets-Sheet 1

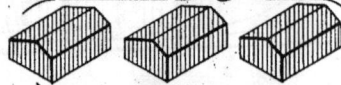

Inventor:
Charles B. Darrow.
by Emey, Booth, Townsend, Motion and Weidner
Attys.

Written Descriptions of the Three Patents:

Please look at the front page of each of the three patents. In all three cases, the general concept is a board game related to the acquisition of real estate. There are commonalities such as a rectangular board layout, and the appearance of certain playing squares (i.e., jail, parking, railroads, and utilities). Nevertheless, there are also marked differences, particularly between Lizzie Magie's patents for the board game she called, "The Landlord's Game", and the patent specifically presenting Monopoly®. The written descriptions in the patents follow the presentations on the first page of each patent. These written descriptions, and the accompanying figures, raise three questions which will be at the heart of this discussion.

The Three Questions Raised from These Patents:

(1) Even though these patents are not identical, are the claims in Lizzie Magie's patents sufficiently broad to cover Monopoly®? Alternatively stated, did all the people who played the game Monopoly® in the 1920's and 1930's infringe Lizzie Magie's patents?

(2) Whether or not there was infringement, do Lizzie Magie's patents bar Charles Darrow's patents by the doctrine of "anticipation"? In other words, could we say that after Lizzie Magie received her patents, Monopoly® was not new, Charles Darrow could not have invented it, and therefore no patent should have been issued to Charles Darrow or anyone else for the game of Monopoly®?

(3) On the basis of the answers to the prior questions, and on a separate review of Charles Darrow's patent US

2,026,082, is US 2,026,082 a litigation-proof patent or not?

Review of the Patents:

Clearly The Landlord's Game is not the same thing as Monopoly®, but they are similar in many respects. The first two questions above are related in that they ask about the impact of Magie's patents on Monopoly®. The first question is, "Are the claims of Magie's patents sufficiently broad so that anyone playing Monopoly® would infringe Magie's patents?" The second question is, "Whether or not Magie's claims are broad, are the written descriptions in Magie's patents sufficiently comprehensive that no patent should have been issued to Darrow?" To answer these questions, we must compare the three patents. Let us compare directly the first claim, #1, for each of the three patents.

The style of claims in the first half of the 20th century is very different from the style of claims today. In the comparison below, I have parsed the claims into elements designated [a], [b], [c], etc., so that a direct comparison is possible. (**Boldface** has been added by me to easily identify the structural elements.)

Table 4–2: Comparison of the First Claims in the Three Monopoly® Patents

	#1: US 748,626	#1: US 1,509,312	#1: US 2,026,082
Inventor	Lizzie J. Magie	Elizabeth Magie Phillips	Charles B. Darrow
Preamble	A game-board	A game-board	In a board game apparatus,

	#1: US 748,626	#1: US 1,509,312	#1: US 2,026,082
Transition	Having	provided with	a board acting as a playing-field having
Element	[a] **corner spaces**, one constituting the starting-point, and	[a] **corner spaces**	
Element	[b] a series of **intervening spaces** indicating different denominations,	[b] **intervening spaces** of spaces of different denominations and values,	[a] **marked spaces** constituting a path or course extending about the board, said path **affording a continuous track** for the purpose of continuity of play,
Element	[c] some of the spaces of the different series corresponding, and distinguished by **coloring or other marking,** so that the corresponding divisions on the four spaces may be readily recognized.	[c] some of the spaces of the different series corresponding, and distinguished by **coloring or other marking,** so that the corresponding divisions on the four spaces may be readily recognized,	[b] certain of said spaces being **designated by position or color so as to constitute a distinguishable group,** there being a plurality of such groups each differing from the others and each having its spaces adjacent on the same side of the board,
Element		[d] a series of **cards** of changeable value, two or more of which are alike and which relate to two or more certain spaces on the board, and	[c] the apparatus having **indications of the rental required** for the use and occupancy, by opponent players, of spaces of one or more such groups,

	#1: US 748,626	#1: US 1,509,312	#1: US 2,026,082
Element		[e] a series of **movable pieces** to be used in conjunction with the spaces on the board	[d] which **rentals are subject to increase by the acquisition of an additional space** or spaces of the same group by the same individual player, thereby making it possible for the possessor to exact greater payments or penalties from any opponent resting or trespassing thereon.
Element		[f] and controlled by **dice**, so as to determine the play.	

General Comments: Lizzie Magie's patents, US 748,626 and US 1,509,312, are extremely similar to one another, particularly in the basic claim elements. The later patent is a refinement, with more elements and hence a narrower scope than the earlier patent. Both of her patents focus on the game board. In contrast, Charles Darrow's patent, US 2,026,082, focuses on a "board game apparatus", which includes two elements — the game board itself, and rental requirements for the various playing spaces. Players of Monopoly® will recall that the game board does not itself include rental requirements — these appear only in the playing cards associated with the properties. In that sense, Darrow's patent truly is "an apparatus" or "system", that includes more than the just the board.

Question (1) — Does Monopoly® Infringe US 748,626 or US 1,509,312?:

US 748,626: This patent makes four of the most common mistakes in patent drafting, and these mistakes limit this patent's scope and usefulness. These problems affect all of the claims, 1–4, but let us focus on claim #1 as an example.

First, common mistake 1 — Unclear Key Claim Terms, appears here. What is meant by "different denominations"? Is the term the same or not the same as "different series"? Is either of these terms equivalent to "corresponding divisions"? None of these terms, "denomination", "series", or "division", are explained in the patent. In fact, the word "denomination" appears in all of the claims, but does not appear anywhere outside of the claims and is not defined or otherwise explained. The word "series" also appears in every claim, but appears only once in the written description, in which the "series of spaces upon the board are colored to distinguish them".[105] The phrase "corresponding divisions" appears in claims 1 and 4, whereas "different divisions" appears in claim #2 and "four divisions" in claim #3. The word "division" never appears outside the claim, although there is a phrase that the board "is divided into a number of spaces and sections and four (4) spaces in the center". To be blunt, no one could possibly understand the exact meaning of these terms — a court might interpret these terms as the patentee desires, but also might not. This is an extremely poor presentation due to a failure to define or otherwise explain the Key Claim Terms in the patent.

Second, common mistake 2 — Roads Not Taken, meaning various embodiments and implementations that might

---

[105] US 748,626, column 2, lines 69–70.

have been presented and claimed, but were not. That mistake appears strongly here in the form of extremely limiting claim language. In claim #1, there are multiple kinds of "spaces", including "corner-spaces", "intervening spaces", and "the four spaces". The only discussion of "four spaces" in the patent is "the four (4) spaces in the center indicating, respectively, 'Bank,' 'Wages,' 'Public Treasury,' and "Railroad.'"[106] That seems to be the intent, which is an accurate description of the game board, but which as a claim element is drastically limiting. To be clear, the game Monopoly® as it appears does not include these "four (4) spaces", and hence, Monopoly® does not infringe claim #1 of US 748,626. This same severe limitation, the "four (4) spaces", destroys the scope of all the claims. Claim #4 is further limited by a recitation of additional claim elements, including "charters" (which are not explained at all in the patent), "legacies" and "luxuries" (neither of which appear in Monopoly® and either of which may be easily avoided). In short, all of the claims of US 748,626 are very narrow in scope, and none of the claims appear to be infringed by Monopoly®.

Third, common mistake 6 — Lack of Claim Mix. There is no claim mix whatever in US 748,626. All of the claims are for "a game-board". This lack of mix is somewhat bewildering, given that the essence of the game is to play it. One would think that there would be method claims in this patent, but there are not.[107] Any person wishing to avoid infringement

---

106   US 748,626, column 1, lines 29–32.

107   See footnote 101 above. A patent claim for a method of playing a game would not have been filed in the early 1900's, nor would such a claim have been allowed by the patent office. Therefore, the "bewilderment" at the absence of such a claim occurs only for modern evaluators. In modern eyes,

needs only to avoid a bit of the very detailed structure set forth in the claims. This is not a difficult task.

Fourth, common mistake 8 — Improper Use of Non-Standard Terminology. Of the four claims in this patent, half of them use the transitional phrase "having", and half of them use the transitional phrase "provided with". Both phrases are non-standard. Also, why are there two different transitions? What does the difference mean? Were this patent to go to court, a defendant would have many opportunities to interpret the claims narrowly so as to avoid liability.

The other internal common mistakes are apparently not made in this patent. No external events that destroy patent value are evident.

US 1,509,312: There are five claims in this patent, and they have exactly the same problems as the claims in Lizzie Magie's earlier patent.

The same Key Claim Terms are undefined and unclear.

The claims add additional elements that restrict severely the scope of the patent, and probably exclude all infringement. For example, there is a "chance cube" in claims 2–5 that alters the results of the dice, that does not exist in Monopoly®, and that could easily be omitted by a copycat manufacturer in order to avoid infringement — the copycat could produce the same game, but without the "chance cube". For example, claim #3 includes "franchises", claim #4 includes "foreign ownership of American soil", and claim #5 includes "no trespassing signs", none of which exist in Monopoly®, and any of which could be omitted from a copycat game to avoid infringement.

---

the absence of method claims is a weakness in this patent, but such absence surely was not a mistake by the writers of the patent.

All of the claims are again for "a game-board". There is no claim diversity.

All of the transitional phrases in the claims are "provided with".

Lizzie Magie invented The Landlord's Game, for which great deference is due. The two patents she obtained seem to cover The Landlord's Game as she invented it, but these patents are not sufficiently broad to cover Monopoly® or any other serious competitor of The Landlord's Game.[108] No player of Monopoly® infringed either of Magie's patents.

Question (2) — Do Lizzie Magie's Patents Bar Charles Darrow's Patent as Being "Not New"?:

US 2,026,082: There are nine claims in Charles Darrow's patent, US 2,026,082. The structure of these claims is a bit unusual. In the first half of the 20th century, claims in U.S. patents are predominantly in the independent form — that is, in many early patents, all of the claims are written as independent claims. For example, all of the claims in all three of the Monopoly® patents discussed here are in the independent form. Nevertheless, by the copying of specific elements in specific claims, we can discern which claims were considered by the patentee to be truly independent, and which were dependent in the sense that they are simply narrower than the other claims. Here, the claims that are really independent

---

[108] This conclusion is not dependent on the way things are done in 1904, 1924, or today in 2014. The essential problem in Magie's two patents is that the Key Claim Terms appear to be undefined, unclear, and very narrow. This problem is not time-dependent, nor is it related to the way patent writing has changed in the last 100 years. The claims here may cover The Landlord's Game, but they are unlikely to cover anything else.

are #1, #6, #7, #8, and #9. The apparent claims sets are made of claims 1–2–3 (independent claim #1, claim #2 dependent on #1, and claim #3 dependent on #2) and 6–5–4 (independent claims #6, narrower claim #5 dependent on claim #6, and narrower claim #4 dependent on claim #5). Each of the other claims, #7, #8, and #9, also appears to be independent. If these claims were written today, in the 21st century, their probable order would be claim set 1–2–3, then claim set 6–5–4, then independent claims #7, #8, and #9.

The independent claims are very good, in that they describe clearly the essence of Monopoly®, and would prevent a competitor from making a copycat product.[109] The claims do not cover a "board", but rather an "apparatus", which they explain to be a board plus one or more other things. Claim #1, for example, has four elements, but these elements present two different ideas. The first idea, presented by elements [a] and [b], is a board with continuous spaces around the outer edge, in which some spaces that are adjacent to one another are grouped by color. The only serious limitation in this element is the phrase, "adjacent on the same side of the board", which is exactly how property groups appear in Monopoly®, but which a copycat manufacturer could avoid by shifting property groups such that they appear on at least two sides of the board.[110] This element is very similar to the concepts pre-

---

[109] A copy of some sort can always be made, and that cannot be prevented, but the essential features of Monopoly® could not be presented in a competing product without infringing this patent. In that sense, US 2,026,082 is a good patent.

[110] By designing a game board such that the properties of any one color appear on two or more sides of the board, a copycat manufacturer avoids this claim element of US 2,026,082. Conversely, the patent owner could still argue for liability under the Doctrine of Equivalents, but this is a difficult

sented in Lizzie Magie's patents — her board is the same shape as the board in Monopoly®, it also has continuous spaces, and her spaces are also colored. It is not clear if Magie's patents include spaces "grouped by color", and that could be debated either way, but apart from that, it would seem that Magie's patents describe elements [a] and [b] in Darrow's patent.

The second idea in US 2,026,082, presented by elements [c] and [d], is "indications of rentals" which vary based on ownership of properties. That is exactly the way Monopoly® works — the "indications of rentals" appear on the property cards, and they vary based on the ownership of a group of properties. Claim #6, for example, not shown here, includes the board (but *without* the severe limitation "on the same side of the board"), "dice or the like", "a set of miniature buildings", and "tokens or symbols...constituting the playing pieces". These elements clearly define what Monopoly® is all about. The phrase "dice or the like" is particularly good patent drafting, since this element is defined in the written description as,

> "Any suitable chance-determining element or means..., such, for example, as the two dice represented at **61** in Fig. 5...[or] any other suitable chance-determining element... as, for example, an arrow or pointer pivoted to be spun..."[111]

It is hard to see how this element could have been explained any better. All three methods for explaining Key Claim Terms are used, that is, an element in a figure plus explanation, a definition ("chance-determining element"),

---

argument to make where the claim #1 specifically says that all properties of one color are "adjacent on the same side of the board". See "Doctrine of Equivalents" in the Glossary.

[111] US 2,026,082, column 3, lines 32–37.

and specific examples (i.e., dice, an arrow, and a pointer). Also, there is nothing in Lizzie Magie's patents that match the idea presented in elements [c] and [d] of US 2,026,082, claim #1. Yes, the board in The Landlord's Game lists different rentals for individual properties, but the key aspect of Monopoly®, which does not appear in The Landlord's Game, is the grouping of specific properties by different colors, with different rents based upon acquiring monopolies over an entire colored group of properties.

Other claims in US 2,026,082, present other ideas that are not present in Lizzie Magie's patents. These include, for example, "chance cards" in claim #2 of Mr. Darrow's patent, and houses and hotels in claim #3 of Mr. Darrow's patent. The claims in US 2,026,082 are not anticipated by and would not be barred by the written descriptions of US 748,626 and US 1,509,312.

Question (3) — Is US 2,026,082 a Good Patent or Not?:

Is US 2,2026,082 a litigation-proof patent or not? All patent evaluations are conducted according to what I have called the VSD method, meaning a review of **V**alidity of claims, **S**cope of claims, and **D**iscoverability of infringement.[112] The scope of the claims, as explained above, is very good. There would

[112] By this I mean that every evaluation of a patent, without exception, includes all three and only these three criteria. Are the claims valid? Do they have a good scope? Could infringement be discovered? Sometimes an issue is not presented only because it is assumed — for example, an evaluator may assume that claims are valid, or may assume that infringement can be seen. But such an assumption does not change the fact that some kind of evaluation was made. Many evaluation systems break these three criteria into multiple sub-criteria, and I have therefore seen evaluations with many more factors. Different criteria can be assigned to different weights. Many

be no problem with discovering infringement, since it can be observed easily by anyone who obtains a version of the infringing product. In both scope of coverage and discoverability of infringement, US 2,026,082 is a very good patent. However, there is a serious problem with the Validity of the claims, as explained below.

From an internal perspective, the claims appear to be valid. The earlier patents by Lizzie Magie do not include all of the element in the Darrow patent, so the Darrow claims would appear to be "new". Of course, one could also argue that the Darrow claims are "obvious" in light of Magie's claims, so the claims in US 2,026,082 should not have been granted. But it is the job of the U.S. PTO to review prior patents, and it is very unlikely that the U.S. Patent Office would have missed the earlier patents over board games. Moreover, every claim in every issued patent is presumed to be valid by 35 United States Code sec. 282, and invalidity must be proved by "clear and convincing evidence", a very heavy burden of proof. On their face, the claims of Darrow's patent US 2,026,082 appear to be valid.

Further, it seems that US 2,026,082 does *not* commit the most common patent mistake of unclear KCTs. This is a big contribution to patent quality, and a major contribution to the value of the patent.

However, this patent does suffer from other internal mistakes.

First, common mistake 2 — Roads Not Taken. The patent is extremely narrow, focused specifically on the game of Monopoly® exactly as that game has come to be known. The

---

variations are possible for evaluation systems and methodologies. All of this is explained in great detail in Chapters 2 and 7 of *TPV*.

game of Monopoly® is certainly covered, but probably no other game or variation is covered.

Second, all of the claims relate to "a board game apparatus". Why are there no claims for the method of playing monopoly? This is common mistake 6 — Lack of Claim Mix.[113]

Third, non-standard terminology is used, common mistake 8. Six of the nine claims use the non-standard transitional phrase "including", and three of the claims (claims #1, #2, and #3) lack a transitional phrase, using only the preamble "In a game board apparatus", and merely assuming some word such as "including" or "having" or even "comprising".

These three internal mistakes detract from the quality of the patent, but the mistakes are not fatal to the claims, and overall US 2,206,082 appears to be a good patent.

The main problem, however, is not internal to the patent, but rather external. The main problem is what I have called common mistake 10 — External Events that Destroy Patent Value.[114] In this case, the question is, "Who actually invented Monopoly®?" Was it Charles B. Darrow? If so, was he the sole inventor? Under 35 United States Code sec. 101, "Whoever invents…may obtain a patent therefor…" If Darrow was not an inventor at all, then the patent violates section 101, and should never have issued. Further, by law the inventor must issue an oath stating he is the true or joint inventor, 35 United States Code sec. 115 for sole inventor and sec. 116 for joint inventor. If Darrow knew that he was not an inventor, or if he knew there were other inventors whom he did not include

---

[113] See footnotes 101 and 107, above.

[114] This concept is defined in the Glossary below, and is discussed extensively in Chapter 5 of *TPV*.

on the patent, then his oath was fraudulent, and again, the patent is invalid.

Who invented Monopoly®? Some people have suggested that Lizzie Magie was the true inventor.[115] Although this might be possible, it is very difficult to reach this conclusion on the evidence of her two patents. The Landlord's Game does indeed include a four-sided board game based on monopoly over real estate, but very many of the specific elements in the Monopoly® and in US 2,026,082 are not revealed or implied in Magie's two patents. In a colloquial sense, perhaps, one could say that Lizzie Magie "invented" the general concept of a monopoly-like game, but there is not sufficient evidence to say she invented the game called Monopoly®.[116]

However, other people have suggested that Charles Darrow

---

[115] See, for example, David W. Brown, "Reobituaries: Elizabeth 'Lizzie' Magie, Inventor of Monopoly", *Mental Floss*, (February 6, 2013); "Charles Darrow", Wikipedia; and Mary Pilon, "Monopoly Goes Corporate", *New York Times Sunday Review*, (August 24, 2013). All of these articles say that Lizzie Magie was the sole inventor. That might be true, but only in the layman's sense that she created the general concept. However, her patents do not bar (that is, they do not "anticipate") the claims in Darrow's patent. Lizzie Magie might have been one inventor of the game, but almost certainly she was not a sole inventor. Other sources do suggest that Lizzie Magie was one of several inventors of the game. For example, the Wikipedia entry for "Monopoly (game)", states that Lizzie Magie and Charles Darrow were the two "designers" of the game. All of this is interesting intellectually, but not practically. If Darrow was not the sole inventor of the game and he knew that, then he committed fraud against the patent office, his patent should not have been granted, and the patent would have become unenforceable as soon as the fraud was discovered.

[116] In the world of patents, a person is "an inventor" if he or she contributed to one or more of the claims of a patent. See, e.g., *Ethicon, Inc. v. United States Surgical Corp.*, 135 F. 3d 1456, (Fed. Cir. 1998), at p.1460. A person is a "sole inventor" only if that person was the sole contributor to all of the claims of the patent. This definition is very much different from the common understanding of the word "inventor".

received the entire game from other people.[117] If this allegation is true, then he is not an inventor at all, or at best he is one inventor of multiple other inventors whom he did not invite to join on the patent. If this allegation is true, then Darrow's dishonest oath of ownership would constitute fraud against the PTO, in which case US 2,026,082 would be unenforceable, and therefore, in essence there would be no valid patent for Monopoly®.

Let us summarize what has been said here in an illustrative table.

Table 4–3: Review of Charles Darrow's Monopoly® Patent US 2,026,082

	Internal	External
Validity of Claims	YES	NO (apparently)
Scope of Coverage	YES	Not Relevant
Discoverability of Infringement	YES	Not Relevant

---

[117] Apparently Louis Thun, co-inventor in 1932 of a game called "The Fascinating Game of Finance", told the President of Parker Brothers that he had been playing the monopoly game, in the form later adopted by Darrow, since 1925, so Darrow could not have been the inventor of the game when his patent application was filed in 1935. Mary Bellis, "Monopoly, Monopoly, Part I: The History of the Monopoly Board Game and Charles Darrow", *About. com*, (February 22, 2012). According to Ralph Anspach, a retired economics professor and creator of the game "Anti-Monopoly", the inventors of the game Monopoly® were Lizzie Magie, who invented the general concept, and a group of Quakers in Atlantic City, New Jersey, who added the specific features later adopted by Darrow. "Anti-Monopoly", Wikipedia. See also the Wikipedia entry for "Charles Darrow", where it is stated that Charles Todd taught Darrow the "virtually identical" version of the game that Darrow later patented. In short, there are many allegations, although the truth of the allegations is not clear.

Charles Darrow might not have been the inventor of Monopoly®, or if he was an inventor, then he may have been only one of multiple inventors. If it is true that he was not the sole inventor of the game, if he knew that, and if he deliberately withheld this information from the U.S. Patent Office, then there has occurred an "external event that destroys patent value", and all of the claims of US 2,026,082 would be unenforceable due to fraud against the patent office.

CONCLUSION ABOUT THE MONOPOLY® PATENTS:

To answer the three questions, (1) no, the players of the game Monopoly® did not infringe the claims of Lizzie Magie's patents; (2) no, Magie's patents do not "anticipate" (that is, they do not make non-novel) Darrow's patent; and (3) US 2,026,082 appears to be an excellent patent for both coverage of Monopoly® and discoverability of infringement, and for that reason, patent US 2,026,082 should indeed give a monopoly over the game of Monopoly®.

This, however, is not the end of the matter. According to a VSD analysis of US 2,026,082, this patent would score very high for **S**cope and **D**iscoverability, but the patent may be useless because none of its claims may be **V**alid, due to what appears to be a deliberately incorrect statement of inventorship. This is an example of an "external event that destroys patent value".

The Monopoly® patent expired in 1952, more than a half-century ago. No court will ever review the allegations presented here, and no court will ever rule on the validity of US 2,026,082. For the truth of these events, all external to the patent, we will need to leave the final conclusion to historians of American business.

❖ ❖ ❖

Example of a Good Patent from Recent Patent Litigation

Introduction:

It seems fitting to summarize this book by reviewing one good patent from a recent patent litigation. I will discuss the patent, focus specifically on the explanation of Key Claim Terms, and then compare this patent against the most common mistakes in patents.

I have selected US 8,046,721, entitled, "Unlocking a device by performing gestures on an unlock image", priority date December 23, 2005, filed June 2, 2009, issued October 25, 2011. This is the so-called "slide to unlock" patent, issued to Apple, Inc., and asserted by Apple as one of a group of patents against Samsung Electronics in Case No. 12-CV-00630-LHK (United States District Court for the Northern District of California, San Jose Division). On May 2, 2014, the jury in this litigation found that Samsung's Admire, Galaxy Nexus, and Stratosphere products had infringed claim #8, that such infringement was "willful", that this claim #8 was not invalid, and that the total damages for infringement of this claim were almost exactly $3M.[118] This patent is a continuation of an earlier patent, US

---

[118] The jury found that Samsung had infringed three patents, but only infringement of US 8,046,721 was found to be "willful". By law, Apple may request enhanced damages for willful infringement, up to three times the actual damages found, so that the maximum possible damage for

7,657,849, which was not asserted in this case by Apple against Samsung.[119] I consider US 8,046,721 to be a very good patent, for reasons explained below. It is also, however, not a perfect patent, also for reasons explained below.

US 8,046,721

Here is the relevant claim #8, parsed by its element components:

Table 4-4: Claim #8 of Apple's Slide to Unlock Patent

Preamble	A portable electronic devise,
Transition	comprising:
[1]	a touch-sensitive display;
[2]	memory;
[3]	one or more processors; and
[4]	one or more modules stored in the memory and configured for execution by the one or more processors, the one or more modules including instructions:
[5]	to detect a contact with the touch-sensitive display at a first predefined location corresponding to an unlock image;

infringement of claim #8 is about $9M. The decision in this case is subject to appeal and other proceedings, but that fact does not alter my opinion of the patent.

119   Apparently the earlier patent, US 7,657,849, has been asserted by Apple against HTC and Motorola, but not against Samsung.

[6]	to continuously move the unlock image on the touch-sensitive display in accordance with movement of the detected contact while continuous contact with the touch-sensitive display is maintained, wherein the unlock image is a graphical, interactive user-interface object with which a user interacts in order to unlock the device; and
[7]	to unlock the hand-held electronic device if the unlock image is moved from the first predefined location on the touch screen to a predefined unlock region on the touch-sensitive display; [and]
[8]	instructions to display visual cues to communicate a direction of movement on the unlock image required to unlock the device.

Key Claim Terms in US 8,046,721

What are likely to be Key Claim Terms in claim #8 above? The essence of the invention here, the "innovative concept" or "Point of Novelty", appears to be a method of unlocking a cell phone, including structure supporting the method (but the structure does not itself appear to be a Point of Novelty, even though claim #8 as drafted is "a portable electronic device"). The KCTs would therefore seem to be in the elements related to instructions, and might include:

— In element 5, "first predefined location";
— In element 6, "continuously move" and "continuous contact";
— In element 7, "predefined unlock region";
— In element 8, "visual cues".

One of the most important aspects of writing a good

patent is to explain the Key Claim Terms. There are three ways to explain KCTs.[120] How does US 8,046,721 use these three methods?

Method 1 to explain KCT — Definition of the term: There is no "definitions section" or anything like it, anywhere in US 8,046,721. A few of the key terms are defined, but not many, and it would be fair to say that the drafter of this patent does not rely extensively on method 1.

Method 2 to explain KCT — Examples of the term: In contrast, the drafter of US 8,046,721 relied very heavily on examples of Key Claim Terms. There are at least 20 different words or phrases that the drafter explains through multiple examples, including terms such as "device", "memory", "network", "input/output devices", "operating system", "application installed on the device", and many others. This is the main method that the drafter used to explain terms in the patent.

Method 3 to explain KCT — Element of a figure plus explanation of the element: Every patent includes figures, elements of the figures, and explanation of the elements. That is also true of US 8,046,721.

According to these three methods, how have the four key terms been explained in the patent?

1. *"First Predefined Location"*: The word "predefined" appears about 90 times in the patent, and modifies nouns such as "location", "gesture", "path", "functions", and others. However, "predefined" itself is not defined. Further, there is no definition of the phrase "first predefined location", nor

---

[120] As has been explained, the fourth way, "claim differentiation", is used by a court to interpret the claims, but should never be relied upon by the patent writer.

any definition of the concept of "the initial location prior to moving the image".

It is important to be exact here. There is an extensive discussion of the concept of "location" in column 11, lines 23–62, including this definition:

"The location(s) may be defined narrowly or broadly, and may be one or more locations on the touch screen, one or more regions on the touch screen, or any combination thereof. For example, the location may be defined as a particular marked location, areas at each of the four corners of the touch screen, or a quadrant of the screen, etc."

This is a very good explanation of "location", since it includes both a definition (method 1 of explaining Key Claim Terms) and examples (method 2 of explaining KCTs). This explanation does not define "predefined location", although perhaps that term could be inferred. A more serious problem, however, is that this quote does not explain "*first* predefined location". The term applies specifically to the "location" *after* movement, what is called in the patent a location "meeting one or more predefined unlock criteria" (column 11, line 37). This definition does not apply to the "location" or position *prior to* movement, what the claims call the "first predefined location".

Although there is no definition of the term "first predefined location", one could argue that the definition of "predefined location" *post*-movement should apply also to the location *pre*-movement, but that is not clear in the patent. This is an error that would never have arisen if there had been a "definitions section" at the start of the Detailed Description,[121] and if

_____

[121] My final opinion is that this is patent is not merely good, but actually very good, meaning the patent is well considered and well written. It is not

the term "predefined location" had been specifically defined in the written description.

There are no examples of "first predefined location" in the patent (as opposed to post-movement location, for which there are examples, as noted above). An "unlock image" in a first position is shown in elements 402, 702, and 1002, in various figures, and perhaps these images are located at the "first predefined location", but "first predefined location" is neither shown nor discussed. The meaning of "first predefined location" must be inferred from the meaning of "location" post-movement.[122]

2. *"Continuously moving"* and *"continuous contact"*: The adjective "continuous" appears 17 times in the patent, including 13 times in the phrase "continuous contact" and 4 times in the phrase "continuously moving". However, there is no definition of "continuous", or "continuous contact", or "continuously moving", and the KCT "continuously moving" appears only in the claims, not in the written description.[123]

---

perfect, however. It would have been better had the Key Claim Terms been identified, and broad definitions applied in a "definitions section" at the start of the Detailed Description. The inclusion of such a "definitions section" occurs in some U.S. patents today, but it is not the common practice. In my opinion, it should be the common practice. See the discussion above, "Writing a Patent Application".

122 The jury in *Apple v. Samsung* apparently did not have a problem with the term "first predefined location", and perhaps they understood the term from the explanation of "location" post-movement. The point, however, is that the phrase "first predefined location" is a Key Claim Term, and the phrase could have been explained much more clearly in the patent.

123 The application as filed included the phrase, "move the unlock image", but did not include the adverb "continuously", which was added during prosecution to all of the independent claims. Since these additions to the claims of the word "continuously" occurred during prosecution, perhaps it is

There are no examples of "continuous contact" in the patent, but "continuous contact" is contrasted with "breaking of the contact" when the motion is complete (column 9, lines 38–39).

FIG. 5B is explained by saying that the user's finger "is in continuous contact with the touch screen 408, in the direction of movement 504." Although "continuous contact" is mentioned, no specific element in the figure represents "continuous contact".

In general, the concept of "continuity", either by "contact" or by "movement", would have been much clearer if there had been a definition of "continuity" or "continuous" in the patent. There is no such definition. There are indications, including contrasting phrases and a discussion of one figure, which apparently were acceptable to the jury in *Apple v. Samsung*. However, the explanations of the Key Claim Terms, "continuously moving" and continuous contact" would have been much stronger with clear definitions of these terms or of at least the word "continuous".[124]

---

understandable that the phrase "continuously move" does not appear at all in the written description. However, the phrase "continuous contact" appears 9 times in the written description without definition or explanation, and this is the crux of the problem. "Continuous contact" is clearly a Key Claim Term, should have been understood as a KCT before the application was filed, and should have been very clearly explained in the written description.

[124] US 8,046,721 is a continuation of the application that eventually became US 7,657,849, which was filed on December 23, 2005. US 8,046,721 incorporates by reference both US 7,657,849, and a related patent application that later became US 7,480,870, also filed on December 23, 2005. All three of these patents make repeated reference to "continuous contact" with either the touch screen or with the "touch-sensitive display", but none of the patents define or otherwise explain "continuous contact", and none of them use the word "continuously" except in the independent claims of US 8,046,721 (which, as noted above, was added during prosecution of US 8,046,721).

3. *"Predefined unlock region"*: This is well defined as the place *after* the movement. See the discussion of "first pre-defined location", above.

4. *"Visual cues"*: This KCT is well explained by examples and figures in elements. Although there is not a formal definition, the function of "visual cues" is to "provide hints or reminders of the unlock action to the user" (column 9, lines 13–14). There are multiple examples of "visual cues", which may be "textual, graphical or any combination thereof" (column 9, lines 14–15). Elements in figures may be "visual cues", such as channel element 404 (described at column 12, line 25), or channel element 1004 and arrow 1006 (described at column 18, lines 4–6).

US 8,046,721 Compared to Common Patent Mistakes

A number of common mistakes in patent writing have been discussed in this book. How did this patent fare in comparison to these mistakes?

As noted, on common mistake 1 — Unclear Key Claim Terms, the patent is relatively good, but there are several terms that are not adequately explained, and this absence creates possible confusion.

On common mistake 2 — Roads Not Taken, the patent appears to be very strong in its direct focus, which is tactile manipulation of an image on a screen from lock to unlock. However, various embodiments that might have been

---

"Continuous contact" was clearly a Key Claim Term in all of these patents, and should have been discussed in some detail.

described and claimed were not, and in that sense, the patent is only adequate in regard to common mistake 2. For example:

a. The patent's discussion of "touch" is not entirely clear. To limit the patent to solely the touch of only a human finger would be very limiting. In fact:

(1) The only apparatus used or demonstrated is a "touch screen",

(2) The word "touch" is used repeatedly, but without a definition. There is a reference to "haptic and/or tactile" at column 5, line 29, but this is not a definition, and frankly, I do not fully understand the difference between "haptic" and "tactile" in this context. Perhaps we could say that "haptic, which may include vibration at a point of contact, is a form of "tactile", but the exact meanings of these two words, and the differences between them, are not clear. In many situations, shades of meaning for two adjectives would make little difference, but in this case, the type of physical contact with the face of a telephone is the essence of the invention, so the lack of clarity is damaging.[125]

---

[125] The problem with a word like "haptic" is that it is both narrow and broad at the same time. On the one hand, the literal definition of the word, "relating to the sense of touch", is a subset of "tactile", so that the word "haptic" seems to be superfluous in the phrase "haptic and/or tactile". On the other hand, "haptic technology" is relatively new and continues to develop, so the exact scope of the word is hard to pin down. The term seems to include at least electro-magnetic waves at different frequencies in response to touch, and would seem to include a more general "simulation of vibration or counter-pressure in response to touch". Does the term include implementations currently being developed, such as holography, audio feedback, and others? US 8,046,721 mentions repeatedly "visual feedback" and "audio feedback" to indicate progress in the act of unlocking the device, but these do not appear to be the same as "haptic holography" or "haptic audio", respectively. Compare a different Apple patent, US 8,378,797, "Method and apparatus for localization of haptic feedback", at column 1, lines 11–14, which defines

(3) There is an excellent list of examples for touch technologies, including "capacitive, resistive, infrared, and surface acoustic wave technologies, as well as other proximity sensor arrays or other elements for determining one or more points of contact with the touch screen", column 5, lines 45–49.

(4) The patent is not limited to the human finger, since it includes "any suitable object or appendage, such as a stylus, finger, and so forth", column 5, lines 61–62.

So it seems to be clear that many different kinds of contact are covered by the patent, with different types of contactors (fingers and styluses), and different kinds of technologies, but all of these contacts require "touch". If the contactor, finger or stylus, were five inches from the screen, would that be "touch"? Ten inches? Any conceivable distance, as long as there is line of sight from the touching device (finger and stylus) and the touch screen? Any conceivable distance between the touching device and the touch screen, even without a line of sight?

Touch technologies clearly include "infrared", which is a strong addition. Do they include "ultrasound"? Although touch technologies include "surface acoustic waves", this would seem to be limited to the acoustic waves on the face of the touch screen, and would seem not to include ultrasound at a distance between the touch screen and the touching device (finger or stylus). If radar were the connecting technology,

---

"haptic" as "touch or tactile sensation" and defines "haptic feedback system" as "selective tactile feedback sensation (such as a vibration or other physical sensation, etc.)". This is not an expansive definition of "haptic", but at least the definition is clear. In contrast, there is no explanation whatever in US 8,046,721, but rather a reliance on an industry term whose current boundaries are unclear, and whose future meaning is, in light of current R&D efforts, uncertain. The use of the word "haptic" in US 8,046,721 presented an opportunity to expand the scope of the invention by definition or other explanation, but the opportunity was not seized.

or some other electrical magnetic signal that bounces back, would that be covered by the patent? This might be included under the phrase "other proximity sensing arrays", but the answer is not 100% clear. There are strengths in the way the patent deals with the concept of "touch", particularly the lists of examples, but expansive definitions would have helped to expand the concept.

The discussion here may seem endless, but it is important to remember that the key innovation in this patent is touch between the screen and a person. Everything in the patent related to that innovation should have been explained very clearly. Some of the Key Claim Terms related to touch are indeed well explained, but others are not.

b. The patent seems to be limited to lock-up and unlock areas which are "predefined". Why must they be predefined? Is not touch technology sufficiently developed so that the user could define his or her own lock-up or unlock areas? This is potentially a serious weakness, since competitors could design around the patent by allowing flexibility of areas on the screen.

c. What about customizing interaction not by movement from one area to another, but rather by biometric data, such as the fingerprint of the user? This also is clearly not covered, although in my opinion this implementation is beyond the scope of the patent, and would need to be covered by different patents.

Overall, an adequate performance on common mistake 2 — Roads Not Taken, although the patent might have been stronger.

Other mistakes common to patents do not appear in this patent. Claim parallelism was not employed — it is always optional, and it might have been used, but it was not, so there was no defective parallelism, common mistake 3. Unnecessary limitations in the written description, common mistake 4, are not apparent, apart from what has been discussed above. There is an excellent claim mix, including method claims, device claims, and computer readable medium claims. Hence, there is no appearance of common mistake 6 — Lack of Claim Mix, or of common mistake 7 — Improper Mix of Elements Within a Claim. There is no non-standard language, common mistake 8, no incorrect reliance on a preamble, common mistake 9, and no known external event that destroys patent value, common mistake 10.

CONCLUSION ABOUT APPLE'S "SLIDE TO UNLOCK" PATENT:

The formal review of a patent ends with an analysis of the three factors **V**alidity of claims, **S**cope of claims, and **D**iscoverability of infringement, or VSD for short. The common mistakes in patents discussed in this book can impact greatly the Validity and Scope of the claims in a patent. In US 8,046,721, these common mistakes were, for the most part, not made, and the presentation of this patent is therefore much superior to that of most patents within the fields of Information & Communication Technologies ("ICT"). For that reason, US 8,046,721 is a suitable patent with which to end this book.[126]

---

126 Certainly I cannot say, and I do not say, that the claims in this patent are valid, or that they have the widest possible scope of coverage. That might

CONCLUSION TO CHAPTER 4

The patents discussed in Chapter 4 illustrate the concept of a "litigation-proof patent", and in particular demonstrate how quality is impaired and value lost when a patent demonstrates the most common mistakes. We can summarize these discussions in Table 4–5. In this Table, "Yes" indicates that the mistake appears in the patent, and "No" indicates that the mistake does not appear in the patent.

---

be true, but I am not an expert in the prior art, so I could not make such a statement. The patent's priority date is December 23, 2005, which pre-dates the iPhone and is relatively early for smartphones generally, but I cannot know if there is other relevant prior art. I can say only that certain mistakes that are common in patents and that may impact the validity of patents appear not to have been made in this patent.

It should be noted that at least one commentator says that the concept of slide to unlock was invented by a Swedish company called Neonode long before Apple started to develop the iPhone. However, Neonode, unlike Apple, did not use a graphical icon that slid in response to the movement of a finger. Was the addition of an icon so "obvious" that a patent should not have been granted to Apple? The commentator believed so, and it is a reasonable opinion, but the jury in *Apple v. Samsung* found claim #8 both valid and infringed. See James Bessen, "The Power of No", *Future Tense*, (December 4, 2013). There is very likely other prior art that could be cited against Apple's patent US 8,046,721, but the patent was granted by the patent office and supported by a trial jury. It is not my task here to judge possible prior art against this patent, and I say only that with a few exceptions, the patent avoids the most common patent mistakes presented in this book.

Table 4–5 Common Patent Mistakes and the Patents in Chapter 4

Common Patent Mistakes	Hedy Lamarr Patent	Monopoly® Patents by Magie	Monopoly® Patent by Darrow	Apple Patent
1. Unclear KCTs	**Yes**, "control station" and "movable craft" are unclear. However, other KCTs are either clear on their face or well-defined.	**Yes**, very poor explanations of KCTs.	**No.** Very clear terms, for the most part. The lack of unclarity is unusual in patents.	**Yes**, several terms undefined, such as "predefined", "continuous", and "touch". Overall, a reasonable performance.
2. Roads Not Taken	**Yes**, land-based control is not described, and two-way communication is not described. However, other options are mentioned and claimed.	**Yes**, the game defined is very narrow, and would not include Monopoly® or much of anything else.	**Yes**, overall only the game of Monopoly® is claimed. The claiming for the game is good, but variations would not be covered.	**Not clear.** Concepts of "touch" seem to be limiting. Spoken embodiments not covered (but may be covered perhaps in another patent). "Predefined" is limiting. The parameters of "touch" are not clear. Generally a good performance, but might have been even stronger.

Common Patent Mistakes	Hedy Lamarr Patent	Monopoly® Patents by Magie	Monopoly® Patent by Darrow	Apple Patent
3. Defective Parallelism	**Yes**, in both claim #1 (transmitter and receiver) and claim #4 (control station and movable craft).	**No**, no clear parallelism of elements.	**No**, no clear parallelism of elements.	**No**.
4. Unnecessary Limitation in the Written Description	**Yes**, brief transmission is "a very important feature of the system".	**No**, although the tremendous detail in the written description is negative.	**No**.	**No**.
5. Improper Use of Claim Differentiation	**No**.	**No**, all claims are independent.	**No**, all claims are independent.	**No**.
6. Lack of Claim Mix	**Yes**, all structure claims, no method claims.	**Yes**, all claims are for "gameboards".	**Yes**, all claims are for "board game apparatus".	**No**.
7. Improper Mix of Elements Within a Claim	**Yes**, each independent claim includes both the transmitter and the receiver.	**No**.	**No**.	**No**.
8. Improper Use of Non-Standard Terminology	**Yes**, "including" in claim #1 (whereas the more appropriate "comprising" is in claim #4).	**Yes**, "having" and "provided with"	**Yes**, "having".	**No**.

Common Patent Mistakes	Hedy Lamarr Patent	Monopoly® Patents by Magie	Monopoly® Patent by Darrow	Apple Patent
9. Incorrect Reliance on the Preamble.	**Yes**, a confused preamble focused on a "system", but the claims are for apparatuses.	**No**, very short and clear.	**Apparently yes**, claim #1 seems to be for a "board", but that is only in the preamble.	**No**
10. External Events that Destroy Patent Value	**Apparently no, but unknown.**	**Apparently no, but unknown.**	**Yes**, major potential problem, with possibly catastrophic consequences.	**Apparently no, but unknown.**
OVERALL	**Good description, weak claims.** Most of the internal common mistakes were made. The technology is great, and the written description is good, but the claims are very weak.	**Very narrow.** These patents are not terrible, but they are extremely narrow — they protect "The Landlord's Game", but they do not cover Monopoly®.	**Very narrow.** A very well-drafted patent that covers Monopoly®, but is probably too narrow to cover other board games. The main problem is an external mistake — serious doubt about the correct inventorship.	**Very good, despite some mistakes.** There are some weaknesses with explanations of KCTs and roads not taken, but overall very good. This patent was written with litigation in mind, and the quality reflects the attention to detail.

These reviews have been performed after-the-fact, on issued patents. In order to obtain the best possible patents, the "litigation-proof" patents, applications should be reviewed to insure that these common mistakes do not appear.

Afterword

The great American humorist, Mark Twain, once said, "Everybody talks about the weather, but nobody does anything about it". The same might be said about the topics of "patent quality" and "patent value". Everybody talks about them. They are clearly "hot" topics, if you will pardon the reference to weather. But even though these are clearly topics of much interest today, very little of significance is done about them. To say, as I have heard on occasion, "We review our patents for quality", or "We cull our portfolio to remove the lower quality items", are simply not answers.

Concrete action should be taken to boost the quality, and hence the value, of patents. The bad news is that, unfortunately, there is great room for improvement. The good news is that, fortunately, there is great room for improvement and we know what to do.

This book has sketched, in four chapters, several main ideas:

- Chapter 1 explains how a patent tells its story, and presents a method by which high-quality patents may be written.
- Chapter 2 identifies and explains the major principles of patent quality.
- Chapter 3 identifies and explains ten of the most common

mistakes in the writing of patents. Methods and techniques to avoid these mistakes are also presented.

- Chapter 4 presents five patents that help illustrate the
  idea of "litigation-proof patents". This particular selection was made to illustrate, through specific examples
  taken from the 20th and 21st centuries, that the form of
  patent will change over time, but the characteristics of
  "litigation-proof patents" and the principles of writing
  good patents do not change.

What is needed is to apply the principles of writing good
patents, and to avoid or remove the common mistakes that
occur time and again in patents. Whether or not we can actually do something about the weather,[127] we certainly can act
to fix patents and to provide the highest possible protection
for our inventions. Now is the time.

---

[127] If one googles the quotation by Mark Twain, one discovers two things.
First, many people complain that we have already done things about the
weather, and we must act to undo these things. I am not an expert in global
warming, I honestly do not know the truth about it, and I only note the
irony that what Mr. Twain felt was unchangeable in the 19th century might
be changeable after all in the 21st century, although perhaps not in the way
Mr. Twain intended. Second, it is surprisingly unclear whether the quotation
attributed to Mark Twain was in fact made by him. The quotation might be
from Mr. Charles D. Warner, a personal friend of Mr. Twain. This, too, is
ironic, I suppose. After the lengthy discussion of the true inventorship of
Monopoly®, and the confusion as to whether the game was invented by Ms.
Magie, or Mr. Darrow, or a group of Quakers in Atlantic City, New Jersey,
we find that the correct attribution of quotations, like the correct attribution
of inventions, must be left, at least in some cases, to the tender mercies of
research historians.

Appendix
List of the Principles in the Book

1. Characteristics of Good Patent Claims

Principle 1: *A short and simple preamble is good.*

Principle 2: *A small number of claim elements is usually good.*

Principle 3: *"General" elements in claims tend to be much better than "specific" elements.*

Principle 4: *A large number of elements might not narrow the claim if the elements are very general.*

2. Key Claim Terms

Principle 5: *Clarity of Key Claim Terms is of vital importance to the value of the patent.*

Principle 6: *Patent litigations are almost always decided on the interpretation of one or a very small number of Key Claim Terms.*

Principle 7: *An attack by a defendant against a claim is*

very frequently an attack against a KCT, and such an attack can be defeated if the patent clearly explains the term.

Principle 8: *However, if a claim term is very clear in the technology, then it does not need to be explained.*

Principle 9: *The process of writing good Key Claim Terms is iterative — pick terms carefully, explain them, review the explanations, possibly add new terms with new explanations, rewrite all explanations, review the rewrites, etc.*

Principle 10: *A Key Claim Term may be defined any or all of three specific ways — (1) explicit definition of the term, (2) examples, and/or (3) an element in a figure plus accompanying explanation.*

Principle 11: *Never use claim differentiation to explain Key Claim Terms.*

3. Types of Claims

Principle 12: *The most basic classification of protection is between structure claims and method claims.*

Principle 13: *Good independent claims produce breadth of coverage. Good dependent claims produce depth of coverage.*

Principle 14: *There are special forms for specific kinds of claims.*

4. Patent Value

Principle 15: *Claim mix adds greatly to the value of a patent.*

Principle 16: *Five factors determine the value of a patent: (1) The market size of the main Points of Novelty; (2) The importance of the technical problem addressed by the patent; (3) The simplicity, clarity, and range of the technical solution to the problem; (4) The priority date of the patent; and (5) The quality of the patent.*

Principle 17: *Value is created by both direct and indirect infringement.*

Principle 18: *Patents that are good (but not great) may also create value.*

Principle 19: *The potential value of a patent may be unlocked in a variety of ways.*

Principle 20: *Patent value should not change whether the patent is acquired for offensive or defensive purposes.*

Principle 21: *The party most likely to be able to realize the potential value of a patent is a party expert in the technology of the patent.*

5. Seminal Patents

Principle 22: *A "seminal patent" (1) has broad market coverage; (2) addresses an important technical problem or issue; (3) provides a technical solution that is an important innovation and perhaps the basis of an entire technical industry; (4) has an early priority date; and (5) has very strong forward non-self citations, or other clear evidence of significant value such as significant licensing royalties, victory in litigation, sale for a significant sum, or placement in a successful patent pool.*

Principle 23: *The strength of a seminal patent cannot overcome major mistakes in the patent.*

Principle 24: *A seminal patent may cover only some implementations, but still be seminal.*

6. Tips for Writing Patents

Principle 25: *The writing of patents must be a creative process.*

Principle 26: *Put the specific parts of a patent only in correct sections of the patent.*

Principle 27: *Write the written description in a way that does not limit the scope of the invention embodiments*

Principle 28: *Be consistent in the use of terminology.*

Principle 29: *Claim parallelism requires parallel language.*

Principle 30: *Tying an invention to one technical standard is extremely dangerous.*

Glossary
(Including Acronyms)

Abstract: See "Parts of a Patent".

Background: See "Parts of a Patent".

BCP: Acronym for "Biological, Chemical, and Pharmaceutical", representing three technology areas based on biology and chemistry, which differ fundamentally from ICT. These areas are sometimes called "the unpredictable arts". Compare with "ICT".

Brief Description: See "Parts of a Patent".

Catastrophic Consequences: These are the impacts on a patent caused by catastrophic failure. Entire claim sets may be invalidated. In some cases, an entire patent may be invalidated or rendered unenforceable. See "Catastrophic Failure".

Catastrophic Failure: Some patent mistakes are so serious that they sweep away entire claim sets, or sometimes entire patents. "Vertical shift" in claim terminology is one such mistake that can cause catastrophic failure. "External events that destroy patent value" are often mistakes, or in some cases simply events beyond the control of the patent owner, that can cause catastrophic failure. Most mistakes in patents, including most of the common mistakes listed in this book, cause only moderate damage to patent quality, but do not invalidate entire claim sets. Categorization of patent consequences as "moderate damage" or "catastrophic failure" is comparable to the categorization of problems with electronic components, which are often classified as either "gradual degradation" or "catastrophic failure". See also "External Events that Destroy Patent Value", "Shifting Terminology", and "Vertical Shift".

Claim: For its role in a patent, see "Parts of a Patent". For its components, see "Parts of a Claim". For different kinds of claims, see "Types of Claims".

Claim Differentiation: This is a doctrine that states that each claim in a single claim set must have its own meaning, or "scope", that differs from the scope of any other claim in the same claim set. (If the scopes were the same, then two claims would be saying exactly the same thing, and that is forbidden by law.) Since claim scope is determined by a court, the court will interpret the claims to give a different scope to each claim in the set. The practical effect is that the court will interpret the claims in a way to make the one independent claim in a claim set broader in scope than each of the dependent claims. Here is an example: Claim #1 is a device to guard the health of "household pets". Claim #23 is, "Claim 1, in which the household pet is a dog". By the doctrine of claim differentiation, claim #1 must include "dog" *and one or more additional animals*. Claim #1 *may not be restricted to only "dogs"*, because that would make claim #1 and claim #23 the exact same thing.

Claim Diversity: Same as "claim mix". See "Claim Mix" and "Types of Claims".

Claim Mix: The variety of claims in a single patent. Also called "claim diversity". One way of judging the quality of a patent is by seeing if there is a variety of claims in the patent. Such variety is called "claim mix," or "claim diversity". When people use the term "claim mix", they are usually referring to the types of claims in the patent, meaning (1) system claims, (2) apparatus or product claims, (3) component claims (which may be a circuit, or a sub-system, or some piece of a machine that performs a particular function), and (4) method claims. This term can also be used in reference to a hardware and software mix of claims, and to a mix of "client-side" and "server-side" claims. The term is also used to refer to a mix of independent claims (which create breadth of claim coverage within a patent) and dependent claims (which create depth of claim coverage). A greater claim mix in a patent is often associated with higher quality, because the same inventive concept can be captured in multiple ways. Good claim mix can mean a broader scope of coverage and a lower chance that all the claims will be invalidated in litigation. See also "Claim Parallelism", and "Types of Claims".

Claim Parallelism: This is a particular kind of claim mix in which a single Point of Novelty is protected by multiple types of claims, and in which the mix is achieved by using the same claim structure and same claim terminology in method and structure claims of the same patent. When done properly, claim parallelism provides very strong protection for a single Point of Novelty. However, claim parallelism requires the same terminology in the various kinds of claims. If different terminology is used, the parallelism is lost, and maximal protection is not obtained. See also "Types of Claims", and "Shifting Terminology".

Claim Scope: Same as "scope of claim". See "VSD Evaluation".

Claim Set: There are independent claims, which do not rely on any other claim, and there are dependent claims, each of which relies on an independent claim. Each dependent claim modifies, and thereby narrows, its corresponding independent claim. One independent claim, plus all the claims that depend on it, are called together a "claim set". Of logical necessity, all the claims in a set are of one type (e.g., method claims, or apparatus claims, or system claims), which is derived from the independent claim.

Claim Validity: Same as "validity of claim". See "VSD Evaluation".

Client-side Claim: See "Types of Claims".

Dependent Claim: See "Types of Claims".

Detailed Description: See "Parts of a Patent".

Detectability of Infringement: Same thing as "discoverability of infringement". See "VSD Evaluation".

Direct Infringement: See "Patent Infringement".

Discoverability of Infringement: Same thing as "detectability of infringement. See "VSD Evaluation".

Divided Infringement: This is a doctrine of patent law which says that all the elements of a patent claim must be practiced by one party for that party to "directly infringe" the claim. If a particular claim requires action by two different parties, the chance of its infringement is very low. In such case, direct infringement can occur only if (1) one of the two parties is the agent of the other party; or (2) one of the parties is controlled by the other party; or (3) the parties collude in some manner that allows a court to attribute the actions of one party to the other party. These three cases do occur, but not often. Therefore, the doctrine divided infringement may reduce drastically the scope of coverage of a particular claim. This doctrine typically has its greatest impact on those method and system claims that include both "client-side" and "server-side" elements. Such claims are rarely infringed. The doctrine is usually much less dangerous for product and component claims which, by their nature, tend to be implemented by a single party. Common mistake 7 — Improper Mix of Elements Within a Claim, is based on the doctrine of divided infringement. Problems of divided infringement may almost always be avoided by drafting each patent claim so that the claim is either wholly "client-side" or wholly "server-side".

"Divided infringement" is also sometimes called "joint infringement", just as the "doctrine of divided infringement" is sometimes called the "doctrine of joint infringement". See also "Patent Infringement".

Doctrine of Divided Infringement: See "Divided Infringement".

Doctrine of Equivalents: Often referenced as the "DOE", this is a legal rule in effect in the United States and in many other countries which says that a defendant may be liable for direct infringement of a patent claim even if the defendant has not done exactly what is included in the elements of the claim. Each country has its own test for the DOE. In the U.S., for example, actions of the defendant may be considered "equivalent" if (1) the differences between such actions and the claim elements are "insubstantial", or if (2) the defendant's actions are considered to perform "substantially the same function" as the claim, "in substantially the same way", and producing "substantially the same results". The Doctrine of Equivalents is a relatively complicated doctrine with its own specific rules, but the bottom line is that in some cases the DOE may expand the scope of liability. See "Patent Infringement".

DOE: See "Doctrine of Equivalents".

Element: See "Parts of a Patent Claim".

External Events that Destroy Patent Value: Even though a patent may have excellent claims and good support in the written description, nevertheless the value of even the best patent can be destroyed by "external events" not related to the patent itself. Examples include (1) failing to file a document on-time; (2) failing to tell the patent office about an important piece of prior art; (3) deliberately listing the wrong inventors on the patent; and (4) not paying renewal fees on-time. These events have nothing to do with the subject matter of the patent, the patent claims, or support for the claims in the written description. These are all "external events that destroy patent value". Such events may, depending on the circumstances, invalidate a single claim, or make a claim unenforceable against one party, or, in the worst case, invalidate *all of the claims* in the patent.

Forward Citation: When prior patent X is cited in later patent Y as being relevant art, patent X has received a "forward citation", because the citation in Y is forward in time relative to the cited patent X. If patent X and patent Y are owned by the same patentee, the forward citation is called a "forward self-citation". If patents X and Y have different owners, the forward citation is a "forward non-self citation". In theory, a "forward citation" may be made in either a patent or a technical paper, but when people say "forward citation", they typically mean only forward citations in later patents.

Forward Non-Self Citation: See "Forward Citation".

Forward Self-Citation: See "Forward Citation".

Horizontal Shift: Also called "horizontal shifting terminology", this is what happens when the usage of a Key Claim Term shifts between different independent claims in one patent. When this happens, "horizontal claim confusion" occurs. The result is that the scope of coverage is less than what the patentee wanted, and, in extreme cases, the confusion may lead to invalidation of patent claims. See also "Claim Parallelism", and "Shifting Terminology". Compare "Vertical Shift".

Independent Claim: See "Types of Claims".

Indirect Infringement: See "Patent Infringement".

ICT: Acronym for "Information & Communication Technologies". Technical areas with patents featuring electronic or mechanical structures or methods, and which tend to be based on applied physics. The group of patents includes computers, electronics, and communication systems — both hardware and software. This group also includes mechanical patents, and also medical device patents (e.g., implants, tools). Material science patents, particularly those in nanotechnology, are also sometimes grouped in ICT. Compare with "BCP".

Information & Communication Technologies: See "ICT".

International Trade Commission: See "ITC".

ITC: Acronym for "International Trade Commission", or "United States International Trade Commission". This is a forum for patent litigation in the United States that is separate from the Federal district courts. A patent owner may sue for infringement in either the ITC or the courts, or in both of them. There are differences between litigation at the ITC and in the courts in terms of procedure, decision-makers, and scope of remedies, all of which are discussed in the earlier book *TRUE PATENT VALUE* at pp. 150–154, but these differences are not relevant for the current book.

Jepson Claim: The American name for what Europeans call the "two-part claim". See "Types of Claims".

Joint Infringement: See "Divided Infringement".

KCT: See "Key Claim Term".

Key Claim Term: Or "KCT", for short. This is an important word or phrase in a patent claim that helps define the meaning or scope of the claim. Often a claim term relates to a specific Point of Novelty in the claim.

Litigation-Proof Patent: A patent that has been written and prosecuted at the patent office in such a way that the issued patent is as strong as it can reasonably be, given the nature of the invention and the technical area of the patent. Another way to look at this is to say that a patent evaluation would rate the patent highly. See also "VSD evaluation". In truth, there is no such thing as a "litigation-proof patent", because unexpected things may always occur in court or ITC litigation, but it is possible to make a patent as "litigation-proof" as it can be. By making a patent litigation-proof in the sense of avoiding the most common patent mistakes, the patent drafter insures that such mistakes cannot detract from the patent's scope of coverage, claim validity, overall quality, or financial value.

Markush Claim: See "Types of Claims".

Method Claim: See "Types of Claims".

Means-plus-function Claim: See "Types of Claims".

Non-Standard Terminology: The usage of new and unique terms for concepts that are already covered by standard terminology. Confusion is almost certain to result. For example, the well-known and standard transitional phrase for ICT patents is "comprising". For some reason, people use non-standard terms such as "having", "including", or "with". This alone is confusing, but if some claims in a patent use "comprising" while others use "including", the confusion is worse. See also "Non-Standard Usage of Standard Terminology".

Non-Standard Usage of Standard Terminology: Usage of an old and well-understood term in a way not intended by the industry most connected to the term. If an industry uses a certain term in some standard way, and a patent uses this same term as part of a claim, but the patent's usage of the term is *not* the same as the industry's usage, confusion is certain to result from such non-standard usage. In such a case, if the patent has presented an explicit definition of the non-standard term, that explicit definition will control the interpretation of the claim. But if there is no explicit definition in the patent, then both claim scope and claim validity will be uncertain. Non-standard usage of standard terminology is not the same as "non-standard terminology". See also "Non-Standard Terminology" and "Shifting Terminology".

Parsing: In the context of patents, "parsing" is the process of breaking a claim into its constituent parts in order to ease a close analysis of the claim. The claim is broken into its three constituent components, the Preamble, the Transition, and the Claim Elements. Further, all of the Claim Elements are enumerated or otherwise designated, so that each element may be easily identified and reviewed. Parsing is often done to analyze the parsed claim, or to compare the parsed claim to another claim (which itself may or may not be parsed). See also "Parts of a Patent Claim".

The concept of "parsing" is used also outside the world of patents, in the sense of a breaking a sentence or an argument into its constituent parts. For example, in Chapter 3, common mistake 9 — Incorrect Reliance on the Preamble, the Federal Circuit Court's explanation of the impact of a claim preamble is parsed into its constituent parts. Here, too, the purpose of "parsing" is to ease a close analysis of the parsed text.

Parts of a Patent: There are a number of specific sections of the patent, any one of which might impact the scope of coverage or validity of the claims. Some, but not all, of the specific sections are described here.

> **Abstract:** A short section that indicates the key Point of Novelty or other key features of the invention.

> **Background:** A discussion of the prior art related to the invention described in the patent. This section often states the deficiencies in the prior art that are solved by embodiments of the invention, but embodiments of the invention should not be discussed in this section.

> **Brief Description:** Very brief descriptions of the figures,

stating only the nature of each figure (method, system, apparatus, etc.) and the figure's general subject. For example, "a flow chart illustrating an embodiment of one method for digital recording". For example, "a top down view of a radio communication device".

Claims: The statements of novelty at the end of the patent that describe what is protected by the patent. The claims are typically preceded by a phrase such as, "I claim:", "We claim:", "What is claimed is:", or the like.

Detailed Description: This section is the heart of the written description. The invention is described in sufficient clarity and sufficient detail that all of the claims of the patent are supported with explanation. In this section, every numbered element of every figure will be noted and explained, however briefly.

Field of Invention: Sometimes called "Field of Technology", or just "Field", this is a very short statement that identifies the general technical area of the patent. Must be broad enough to include both the background technology and the main embodiments of the invention, but not so broad as to invite the application of prior art from technical areas that are either unrelated or tangentially related to the technical area of the embodiments. The Field of Invention is optional, and does not appear in many patents.

Figures: The drawings that (1) show how the invention is built and used, and (2) support all of the structure and method claims. Generally structure claims are supported with structure figures, and method claims are supported with method figures, but, as shown in Table 1–2, each method claim should also be supported by the structure shown in at least one structure figure.

Summary: A summary of all the PONs or key features of the invention. Many patent writers summarize each independent claim in the Summary

Title: The name of the patent. It should be short and descriptive — sufficiently broad to cover the main embodiments of the invention, but not so broad as to invite possible prior art from unrelated or only tangentially related technical areas.

Written Description: As described in 35 United States Code sec. 112(a), the written description includes all the sections of a patent that describe how to make and use the various implementations of the invention, including the invention's structure and method. Multiple structures, and/or multiple methods may be described, in which case they are often called "alternative embodiments". The key sections of the patent included in the written description are the Title, Cross-Reference to Related Applications to establish an early priority date, Field of Invention (which is optional and which often does not appear), Background of the Invention (also called "Related Art"), Brief Summary of the Invention (or simply "Summary"), Brief Description of the Drawings, Detailed Description of the Invention (or "Detailed Description of Preferred Embodiments", or simply "Detailed Description"), and Abstract. The explanation of the patent is called "the written description" and not merely "the description".

The written description includes all parts of the patent except the figures and the claims.

Parts of a Patent Claim: There are three parts to any patent claim, and each part plays a role in creating the quality of the patent. Similarly, to determine the quality and value of a patent claim, an evaluator of the patent must review and consider each part of the claim.

> **Preamble:** This is the phrase at the very start of the claim that mentions the general subject. For example: "A method for distributing a movie..." "A system for protecting data integrity..." "A device for digital communication..."

> **Transition:** Also called "the transitional phase", this is the phrase, usually only one or two words, that comes just after the preamble and just before the elements. For ICT patents, the correct transition between the preamble and the elements is "comprising".

> **Elements:** These are the specific aspects that describe the scope of the claim, and that come immediately after the "transition". It is usually not difficult to identify the elements. Sometimes the elements are denominated, such as (a), (b), (c), etc. Very frequently each element is indented from the left-side margin of the page.

Patent Infringement: There are two kinds of patent infringement, both of which contribute to the value of a patent.

> **Direct Infringement:** When a single party implements all of the elements of one claim, that party is said to

"directly infringe" the claim. The party's actions are "direct infringement".

Indirect Infringement: If a party does not directly infringe, but either (1) "contributes" by knowingly helping another party to infringe, or (2) asks, encourages, or otherwise "induces" another party to directly infringe, then the party that contributes or induces is said to "indirectly infringe"

Patent Pool: Multiple patents that are owned by different parties and aggregated into a single group for joint licensing or litigation are described as being in a "patent pool". A patent pool typically is formed around a written technical standard, and patents admitted to the pool must be, by law, "essential" to implementation of the standard. Because entry into a patent pool follows evaluation by technical and legal experts who have determined that the patent is indeed "essential" to the standard, presence in a pool is one sign of potential value in the patent.

Patent Portfolio: A group or collection of two or more patent items (meaning patents and/or patent applications) that are owned or controlled by the same entity, and that are "related" in the sense that they are directed at the same technical subject or problem. Some people use this term to include all of the patents and applications belonging to a company, whether or not these patent items relate to one or multiple subjects or problems. If, however, the patent items relate to multiple subjects or problems, it would be more accurate to say that the company owns several portfolios, wherein each portfolio addresses a different subject or problem.

Patent Quality: The internal worth of a patent, considering the patent's claims, written description, and the figures supporting the claims. Patent quality is one basis of "patent value", but is not itself patent value. A patent with "high-quality" is as litigation-proof as reasonably possible. Compare "Patent Value".

Patent Value: This is not a measure of "quality", but rather of financial value. Quality is a necessary but not sufficient requirement to maximize value of a patent. A valuable patent is one that is both high-quality and covers current infringement (or covers infringement that will occur in the very near future). If a patent has high quality and also covers significant infringement by major companies, the patent may be worth millions of dollars in financial value through sale, licensing, trading of patent rights, preventing competition during the life of the patent, or for other reasons. Compare "Patent Quality".

Point of Novelty: Abbreviated as "PON", this is the part of the claim that is new, the aspect of a particular claim for which that claim was allowed by an examiner. It is sometimes called "the inventive concept" or "the innovative concept". In every independent claim, there should be only a single PON.

PON: See "Point of Novelty".

Preamble: See "Parts of a Patent Claim".

Prior Art: The structure and method of the way things were done before the invention described in the patent. No invention is created out of thin air — there is no magic in the world of innovation. Invention takes prior art and reorganizes it to create a new and useful thing. Just as the process of inventing involves both the innovation and the prior art on which the invention is based, a patent describes both the invention and the prior art that is changed or reorganized by the invention.

Priority Date: The date on which the patent is considered to have been filed. If the patent does not rely on an earlier filing, then the "priority date" is the date the patent was first filed. If the patent explicitly relies on an earlier patent, then the "priority date" is the filing date of the earlier patent. The priority date is critical for judging the patent claims — a patent claim will be allowed by a patent examiner only if the claim is "new" and "non-obvious" over what has been done immediately before the priority date.

Scope of Claim: Same thing as "claim scope". See "VSD Evaluation".

Seminal Patent: A patent that (1) has broad market coverage; (2) addresses an important technical problem or issue; (3) provides a technical solution that is an important innovation and perhaps the basis of an entire technical industry; (4) has an early priority date; and (5) has very strong forward non-self citations or other clear evidence of significant value such as generating significant licensing royalties, achieving victory in litigation, having been sold for a significant sum in the past, or placement as an "essential patent" in a successful patent pool. See also "Patent Pool".

Server-side Claim: See "Types of Claims".

Shifting Terminology: These are changes in the explanations of one or more Key Claim Terms. Such changes can impact the validity and/or scope of the claims. Changes may occur only in the written description of the invention, or only in the claims, or in both the written description of the invention and the claims. Shifting terminology is never good, and in certain cases the results can be catastrophic. There are several types of shifting terminology, all of which are explained in detail in the earlier book *TRUE PATENT VALUE*. For present purposes, the only relevant types are "horizontal shift" and "vertical shift".

Horizontal shift occurs when two or more independent claims are focused on a single Point of Novelty, but the Key Claim Terms change their form between different claims. For example, in Table 3–1 the independent method claim uses the term "digitized speech samples", but this changes inexplicitly in the independent structure claims to "acoustical signal". Horizontal shift destroys claim parallelism and reduces the scope of claim coverage. At a maximum, horizontal shift can result in the loss of claim parallelism.

"Vertical shift" occurs when a Key Claim Term changes its form or meaning *within a single claim*. The ultimate result of vertical shift is often catastrophic failure, including invalidation of the independent claim in which the shift occurred and of all other claims dependent on that independent claim.

See "Claim Parallelism", "Horizontal Shift", and "Vertical Shift".

Software Claim: See "Types of Claims".

Structural Tag: This term expresses a state of being for an element in a structure claim. It is useful for converting a method into a structure, without combining structural and method elements in the same claim (since a combination of structural and method elements in a single claim is not allowed in patent law). Examples of structural tags include phrases such as, "some structure _____ *configured to* ___", or "some structure _____ *adapted to* _____".

Structure Claim: See "Types of Claims".

Summary: See "Parts of a Patent".

Transition (or "Transitional Phase"): See "Parts of a Patent Claim".

Two-part Claim: The European name for what Americans call a Jepson claim. See "Types of Claims".

Types of Claims: A patent writer may use different kinds of claims to express various Points of Novelty.

> **1. Independent Claims versus Dependent Claims:** A patent must have at least one independent claim, and patents in modern times almost always have multiple dependent claims as well. (In the early part of the 20th century, it was more common for patents to use independent claims for what we would write today as dependent claims.)
>
> > **Independent Claim:** A claim that does not depend on any earlier claim is called "independent". An independent claim will not refer to an earlier claim. An independent claim includes only the elements in that claim itself and, when correctly drafted, includes a single Point of Novelty, although each PON may have multiple independent claims (for systems, methods, hardware, software, etc.). Compare with "Dependent Claim".
> >
> > **Dependent Claim:** A "dependent claim" is a claim

that depends on an earlier claim. Each dependent claim will refer to the earlier claim at the very start. For example, "2. Claim 1, further comprising...", is dependent claim #2, which depends on earlier claim #1. A dependent claim includes all of the elements in the claim depended on, plus at least one element added in the dependent claim. The scope of the dependent claim is necessarily narrower than the claim on which it depends. The dependent claim never comes to life, that is, it does not become operative as a practical matter, unless the claim on which it depends has been rendered invalid or unenforceable. Compare with "Independent Claim".

2. Structure Claims versus Method Claims: Every invention within ICT technologies includes both some kind of structure to allow embodiments or to enable specific actions, and some kind of method for building or using some embodiments. Not every structure and method will be claimed, but every invention has both structures and methods. Although these two types of claims are often discussed in contrast, it should be remembered that the line between structure and method is not always clear. Sometimes, for example, a method claim can easily be converted to a structure claim by using a standard structural tag. For example, if a method step is "processing by a digital signal processor...", the step may be converted into a structural step by saying, "digital signal processor configured to process..."

Structure Claim: A structure claim is a claim in which all of the elements are some kind physical structure. There are various kinds of structure claims, including (1) a system, the largest structure; (2) a product or apparatus; and (3) a component of a product or apparatus, which is the smallest structure. Here, "large" and "small" are not judgmental terms, but simply indicate the relative size and complexity of structure.

Method Claim: In patent law, an inventor may patent a "process". 35 United States Code sec. 101. In the world of patents, the word "process" is not normally used, but rather the resulting claims are called "method claims". These are claims in which every element is an action or step, typically expressed by the -ing form of a verb, such as "storing", or "processing".

3. Client-side Claims versus Server-side Claims: A claim may be entirely client-side, entirely server-side, or a mix of client-side and server-side elements. A claim with mixed elements is very problematic, due to the doctrine of divided infringement. It is therefore very important to understand whether each claim, or more precisely each element in a claim, is "client-side" or "server-side".

Client-side claim: Most communication systems have a client side, sometimes called customer premises, consumer site, mobile station, the home, etc., and a server side. For ICT system and method claims, it is important that you know whether *each element of a claim* is on the client side or the server side. If you have one claim that has both client elements and server elements, that claim is in danger of being invalidated by the doctrine of divided infringement. (Although this danger applies particularly to system and method claims, it is generally not a concern for apparatus or component claims, which, by their nature, are not split between two or more entities.) Compare with "Server-side claim". See also "Divided Infringement".

Server-side claim: Most communication systems have a client side and a server side, the latter sometimes called head end, network operations center, or network control center. For ICT system and method claims, it is important that you know whether *each element of a claim* is on the client-side or the server-side. If you have one claim that has both client elements and server elements, that claim is in danger of being invalidated by the doctrine of divided infringement. Compare with "Client-side claim". See also "Divided Infringement".

4. Hardware Claim versus Software Claim: Hardware and software claims are similar, but not identical, to structure and method claims, respectively. Having a variety of hardware and software claims also increases the claim mix in a patent.

Hardware Claim: In the most basic sense, a "hardware claim" is a claim of a physical structure, and in that sense, "hardware claims" are not distinguishable from "structure claims". However, in some patents, specific functions in a method claim are also considered "hardware", where the function is conducted by a specific piece of hardware. For example, we could say, "a tuner", and that is clearly hardware, but we could also say "tuning a TV signal", and this may also be considered hardware because there is a very specific piece of hardware (i.e., a "tuner"), that performs this function.

Software Claim: A software claim is a claim for the impact of a computer program on the performance of a computer. This is often considered an "algorithm that must be executed by a computer". There is great controversy regarding this type of claim — whether it should be patentable at all, and if so, in what form. Although generally considered to be a method claim, a software claim may also be a structure claim in which each structural element is executing a single step or process of a method. The rules of software patents are country-specific, complex, and frequently changing.

5. Special types of claims:

Jepson = two-part: A Jepson claim is one in which there is a long preamble of prior art, a transition saying "wherein the improvement comprises", and a single element stating an improvement in the prior art. In the U.S., everything in the preamble of a Jepson claim is conclusively and irrefutably presumed to be prior art against the claim. For that reason, the Jepson claim is severely disfavored in the U.S. This same type of claim is called a "two-part form" in Europe, but in Europe the preamble is typically not considered prior art against the claim, and as a result, this form is used quite extensively in Europe.

Markush: This is an element of a claim in which the element is defined as one item from a group of listed items. For example, "an electronic device selected from the group consisting of a computer, a mobile reader, a cellular phone, and a land mobile radio". The advantage of this claim is that it would cover all of the stated implementations — in the example given, each of a computer, reader, phone, and radio, would be covered by this element of the claim. One disadvantage of such a claim element is that if the prior art covers any one of the alternatives, the entire claim element is considered "prior art" and the claim may fall. Instead of a Markush claim, the same effect may be achieved by writing multiple claims, in which each claim is a different example from the Markush group. Writing multiple claims will avoid the vulnerability of a Markush claim, but will generate many claims and can therefore incur relatively heavy filing fees with the patent office.

Means-plus-function: Means-plus-function is an element of a claim in which a technical function is presented as a structure. The standard format is, "means for ____ing _____". This format applies to each individual element of the claim rather than the claim itself, although in common parlance, the phrase "means-plus-function" claim is often used as a short hand to say, "a claim with one or more means-plus-function elements". This format is specifically permitted by 35 United States Code sec. 112(f). However, judicial doctrine requires that the scope of this format be limited solely and strictly to the specific structure described in the written description. For that reason, the means-plus-function format is quite narrow, and tends to be used infrequently in modern American patents.

Validity of Claim: Same as "Claim Validity". See "VSD Evaluation".

Vertical Shift: Also called "vertical shifting terminology", this is what happens when the usage or meaning of a Key Claim Term shifts *within a single claim*. "Vertical claim confusion" then occurs, and the result is often catastrophic failure of claim sets or even the entire patent. See also "Claim Parallelism", and "Shifting Terminology". Compare "Horizontal Shift".

VSD Evaluation: Patents are evaluated by many people, for many purposes. A full evaluation will necessarily include exactly three general criteria, and will try to answer three specific questions: Are the claims **V**alid? What is the **S**cope of coverage afforded by the claims? Is infringement reasonably **D**iscoverable?

> **Validity of claims:** Claims that have been allowed by the Patent & Trademark Office are entitled to a *presumption* of validity, but that does not mean the claims would indeed be valid if placed in dispute. Validity is often challenged at the patent office, in court litigation, and in ITC litigation. Challenges may be based upon problems internal to the patent, on prior art that was not considered by the patent examiner, or on external events

that may invalidate patent claims. If a review of validity does not appear in a formal valuation, it is almost certainly because the evaluator assumes the claims to be valid. Some evaluation systems score claims as either "likely valid" or "likely invalid" — in such an evaluation system, claims that are "likely invalid" might be ignored completely.

Scope of claim coverage: The degree to which a claim covers various products, methods, markets, and companies. Extensive coverage is considered a "broad scope", as opposed to a limited or "narrow scope". People often refer to a patent's "scope of coverage", and in this sense, they mean the coverage for all of the claims in the patent rather than the scope of one particular claim. In contrast to validity, which is often scored on a yes-no scale, scope of claim is usually evaluated with a numerical score indicating a relative degree of coverage

Discoverability (or detectability) of infringement: If infringement of a claim cannot be discovered, there is very little value to that claim. If this is true of all the claims in a patent, the entire patent may be valueless. Most patents do not have a problem with discoverability, but if there is such a problem, it may well dramatically impact the value of the patent.

Written description: See "Parts of a Patent".

Bibliography

Bellis, Mary. "Monopoly, Monopoly: Part 1: The History of the Monopoly Board Game and Charles Darrow", *About.com.*, (February 22, 2012), available at http://inventors.about.com/library/weekly/aa121997.htm, (last viewed September 1, 2014).

Bessen, James, "The Power of No", *Future Tense*, (December 4, 2013), available at *http://www.slate.com/articles/technology/future_tense/2013/12/the_simple_fix_that_could_heal_the_patent_system.html* (last viewed September 1, 2014).

Bessen, James E., "The Value of U.S. Patents by Owner and Patent Characteristics", *Boston University School of Law Working Paper no. 06–46*, pp.1–36 (2006), available at http://papers.ssrn.com/sol3/papers.cfm?abstract_id=949778 (last viewed September 1, 2014).

Brookings Institution — The Metropolitan Policy Program, "Patenting Prosperity: Invention and Economic Performance in the United States and its Metropolitan Areas", Washington, D.C., February, 2013, available at www.brookings.edu/~/media/Research/Files/Reports/2013/02/patenting%20prosperity%20rothwell/patenting%20prosperity%20rothwell.pdf, (last viewed September 1, 2014).

Brown, David W., "Reobituaries: Elizabeth 'Lizzie' Magie, Inventor of Monopoly", Mental Floss, February 6, 2013, available at http://mentalfloss.com/article/48787/retrobituaries-elizabeth-lizzie-magie-inventor-monopoly, (last viewed September 1, 2014).

Carroll, Lewis, *Alice's Adventures in Wonderland*, (Macmillan, London, 1865), often shortened to *Alice in Wonderland*.

Dodson, Edward J., "How Henry George's Principles Were Corrupted into the Game Called Monopoly", December, 2011, available at http://www.henrygeorge.org/dodson_on_monopoly.htm (last viewed September 1, 2014).

Doyle, Arthur Conan, "Silver Blaze", appearing in the collection *The Memoirs of Sherlock Holmes*, (1892).

European Patent Convention, section 43(1).

Fish, Robert D., *Strategic Patenting*, (Trafford Publishing, Victoria, British Colombia, Canada, 2007).

Fish, Robert D., *White Space Patenting: Patenting Ideas, Not Just Inventions*, (Fish & Associates, Irvine, CA, November, 2013).

Freepatentsonline.com, freely accessible electronic database of United States patents, United States patent applications, European patents and applications, English-language abstracts of Japanese patents and applications, English-language WIPO international applications known as "PCT", and German patents and patent applications in the original German. The patents reviewed here are:

— US 748,626, http://www.freepatentsonline.com/07486265.pdf;

— US 1,509,312, http://www.freepatentsonline.com/1509312.pdf; and

— US 2,026,082, http://www.freepatentsonline.com/2026082.pdf.

Gambardella, Alfonso; Harhoff, Dietmar; and Verspagen, Bart, "The Value of European Patents", *European Management Review*, Vol. 5, pp.69–84, (2008), available at http://iprwatchonline.com/uploadfile/201102/20110212122807879.pdf, (last viewed September 1, 2014).

Gambardella, Alfonso; Giuri, Paola; Mariani, Myriam; Giovannoni, Serena; Luzzi, Alessandra; Magazzini, Laura; Martolini, Luisa;

and Romanelli, Marzia, "The Value of European Patents: Evidence from a Survey of European Inventors: Final Report of the PatVal EU Project", European Commission (2005), available at http://ec.europa.eu/invest-in-research/pdf/download_en/patval_mainreportandannexes.pdf, (last viewed September 1, 2014).

Goldstein, Larry M., *Patent Portfolios: Quality, Creation, and Cost*, (True Value Press, Memphis, TN, 2014).

Goldstein, Larry M., *True Patent Value: Defining Quality in Patents and Patent Portfolios*, (True Value Press, Memphis, TN, 2014).

Goldstein, Larry M., and Kearsey, Brian N., *Technology Patent Licensing: An International Reference on 21st Century Patent Licensing, Patent Pools and Patent Platforms*, (Aspatore Books, a division of Thomson Reuters, Boston, MA, 2004).

Hadzima, Joe, of IP vision, "Patent Due Diligence: Strategic Patents & Acquired Liability in M&A", (2014), available at http://web.ipvisioninc.com/IPVisions/bid/34324/Patent-Due-Diligence-Strategic-Patents-Acquired-Liability-in-M-A, (last viewed September 1, 2014).

iRunway, "Patent & Landscape Analysis of 4G — LTE Technology", (2012), available at http://www.i-runway.com/images/pdf/iRunway%20-%20Patent%20&%20Landscape%20Analysis%20of%204G-LTE.pdf, (last viewed September 1, 2014).

Lemley, Mark, "The Limits of Claim Differentiation", Berkeley Technology Law Journal, Volume 22, 1389–1401 (2007), available at http://scholarship.law.berkeley.edu/cgi/viewcontent.cgi?article=1713&context=btlj, (last viewed September 1, 2014).

Pantros IP, "Patent Factor Reports", (2013), available at http://admin.patentcafe.com/reports/pantrosip_reports/patentfactor_terms.pdf, (last viewed September 1, 2014).

Patent Litigation:

Apple Inc. v. Samsung Electronics Co., Ltd., Case No. 12-CV-00630-LHK (verdict on May 2, 2014).

Ethicon, Inc. v. United States Surgical Corp., 135 F. 3d 1456, (Fed. Cir. 1998).

i4i Limited Partnership v. Microsoft Corporation, 670 F.Supp.2d 568 (E.D.Tx. 2009), *affirmed* 589 F.3d 1246 (Fed. Cir. 2009), *withdrawn and superseded on rehearing*, 598 F.3d 831 (Fed. Cir. 2010), *affirmed* 131 S.Ct. 2238, Slip Opinion 10–290 (2011).

Intirtool, Ltd. v. Texar Corporation, 369 F.3d 1289 (Fed. Cir. 2004).

Limelight Networks, Inc. v. Akamai Technologies, Inc., et. al, Case 12–786, 134 S.Ct. 2111 (June 2, 2014)

TiVo, Inc. v. EchoStar Corp., 516 F.3d 1290 (Fed. Cir. 2008), *cert. denied*, 129 S.Ct. 306 (2008).

Trend Micro, Incorporated v. Fortinet, Inc., "In the Matter of Certain Systems for Detecting and Removing Viruses or Worms, Components Thereof, and Products Containing Same", U.S. International Trade Commission ("ITC") Case No. 337-TA-510 (July, 2007).

Uniloc USA, Inc. and Uniloc Singapore Private Ltd. v. Microsoft Corporation, 632 F.3d 1292 (Fed. Cir. 2011).

Pilon, Mary, "Monopoly Goes Corporate", New York Times, August 24, 2013, available at http://www.nytimes.com/2013/08/25/sunday-review/monopoly-goes-corporate.html, (last viewed September 1, 2014).

Quote Investigator (Exploring the Origin of Quotes), "Everybody Talks About the Weather, But Nobody Does Anything About It: Mark Twain? Charles Dudley Warner?", April 23, 2010, available at http://quoteinvestigator.com/2010/04/23/everybody-talks-about-the-weather/ (last viewed September 1, 2014).

Rich, Giles S., "The Extent of the Protection and Interpretation of Claims — American Perspective", 21 *Int'l Rev. Indus. Prop. & Copyright L.*, 497, 499 (1990).

United States Code, Title 35 (also known as United States Patent Act of 1952, as amended):

  35 United States Code sec. 101

  35 United States Code sec. 112(a)

  35 United States Code sec. 112(b)

  35 United States Code sec. 112(f)

  35 United States Code sec. 115

  35 United States Code sec. 116

  35 United States Code sec. 271(a)

  35 United States Code sec. 271(b)

  35 United States Code sec. 271(c)

  35 United States Code sec. 282

United States Patent & Trademark Office:

  Database of recorded patent assignments, http://assignments.uspto.gov/assignments/q?db=pat.

  Database of US Patent Full-Page Images, http://patft.uspto.gov/netahtml/PTO/patimg.htm.

  Ex Parte Reexamination of U.S. Patent No. 5,623,600, Request by Fortinet, Inc., U.S. PTO Control No. 90/011,022, decision of July 17, 2012, Ex Parte Reexamination Certificate issued December 17, 2012, (both the decision and the certificate available on the U.S. PTO's Public PAIR system).

  Glossary Initiative — a pilot program for defining and understanding claim terms, launched June 2, 2014. See www.uspto.gov/patents/init_events/glossary_initiative.jsp (last viewed September 1, 2014).

  Manual of Patent Examining Procedure, section 2111.02 "Effect of Preamble", available at http://www.bitlaw.com/source/mpep/2111_02.html (last viewed September 1, 2014).

United States Patent Act of 1790: Section 1

United States Patents:

  US 748,626, "Game-Board", originally assigned to the inventor Lizzie J. Magie, issued 1903.

US 1,509,312, "Game Board", originally assigned to the inventor Elizabeth Magie Phillips, issued 1923.

US 2,026,082, "Board Game Apparatus", originally assigned to the inventor Charles B. Darrow, subsequently assigned to Parker Brothers, Inc., issued 1935.

US 2,292,387, "Secret Communication System", originally assigned to the inventors Hedy Markey Kiesler (known as "Hedy Lamarr") and George Antheil, issued 1942.

US 5,414,796, "Variable rate coder", original assignee Qualcomm, Inc., issued 1995.

US 5,606,539, "Method and apparatus for encoding and decoding an audio and/or video signal, and a record carrier for use with such apparatus original assignee U.S. Philips Corporation", issued 1997.

US 5,606,609, "Electronic document verification system and method", original assignee Scientific Atlanta, subsequently acquired by Smiths Industries Aerospace & Defense Systems, subsequently acquired by Silanis Technology, issued 1997.

US 5,623,600, "Virus detection and removal apparatus for computer networks", original assignee Trend Micro, Inc., issued 1997.

US 5,774,670, ""Persistent client state in a hypertext transfer protocol based client-server system", original assignee Netscape Communications Corporation, subsequently acquired by AOL, Inc., subsequently acquired by Microsoft Corporation, issued 1998.

US 5,787,449, "Method and system for manipulating the architecture and the content of a document separately from each other", original assignee Infrastructures for Information Inc. ("i4i"), issued 1998.

US 6,233,389, "Multimedia time warping system", original assignee TiVo, Inc., issued 2001.

US 6,714,983, "Modular, portable data processing terminal

for use in a communication network", original assignee Broadcom Corporation, issued 2004.

US 6,885,875, "Method and radio communication system for regulating power between a base station and a subscriber station", original assignee Siemens Aktiengesellschaft, issued 2005.

US 7,480,870, "Indication of progress towards satisfaction of a user input condition", original assignee Apple, Inc., issued 2009.

US 7,657,849, "Unlocking a device by performing gestures on an unlock image", original assignee Apple, Inc., issued 2010.

US 8,046,721, "Unlocking a device by performing gestures on an unlock image", originally assignee Apple, Inc., issued 2011.

US 8,378,797, "Method and apparatus for localization of haptic feedback", originally assignee Apple, Inc., issued 2013.

US 8,771,184, "Wireless medical diagnosis and monitoring equipment", original assignee Body Science, LLC, issued 2014.

US 8,786,495, "Frequency channel diversity for real-time locating systems, methods, and computer program products ", original assignee Zebra Enterprise Solutions Corp., issued 2014.

US 8,812,702, "System and method for globally and securely accessing unified information in a computer network", original assignee Good Technology Corporation, issued 2014.

Wikipedia, "Anti-Monopoly", (last viewed on September 1, 2014).

Wikipedia, "Charles Darrow", (last viewed September 1, 2014).

Wikipedia, "George Antheil", (last viewed September 1, 2014).

Wikipedia, "Hedy Lamarr", (last viewed September, 2014).

Wikipedia, "History of the board game Monopoly", (last viewed September 1, 2014).

Wikipedia, "Monopoly (game)", (last viewed September, 2014).

Index of Figures and Tables

Index of Names and Subjects

V

W

About the Author

Larry M. Goldstein is a U.S. patent attorney specializing in Information & Communication Technologies. He evaluates patent quality, manages patent portfolios, and is engaged actively in the drafting and prosecuting of patent applications. He is the author *PATENT PORTFOLIOS: Quality, Creation, and Cost* (2014); *LITIGATION-PROOF PATENTS: Avoiding the Most Common Patent Mistakes* (2014); and *TRUE PATENT VALUE: Defining Quality in Patents and Patent Portfolios* (2013). He helped establish the patent pool for FRAND licensing of 3G Wideband CDMA technology, and he is a co-author of the book *TECHNOLOGY PATENT LICENSING: An International Reference on 21ˢᵗ Century Patent Licensing, Patent Pools and Patent Platforms* (2004). Mr. Goldstein holds a B.A. from Harvard College, an MBA from the Kellogg School of Management at Northwestern University, and a J.D. from the University of Chicago Law School. His web site is www.truepatentvalue.com.

www.ingramcontent.com/pod-product-compliance
Lightning Source LLC
Chambersburg PA
CBHW061209220326
41599CB00025B/4576